More Memories
of
Middlesbrough

The publishers would like to thank the following companies for their

support in the production of this book

Main Sponsor

University of Teesside

Atha & Co

Reg Boyle Bookmakers

Cherry Hill Nurseries & Garden Centre

Clinkard Group

AV Dawson

David Fox Transport

Greco Brothers Limited

Jack Hatfield Sports

Hills' Interiors & Construction

Park Lane Garage

Parson & Crosland

SM Thompson

WB Robinson & Sons Limited

First published in Great Britain by True North Books Limited
England HX5 9AE
01422 377977

ISBN 1 903204 42 9

Text, design and origination by True North Books Limited
Printed and bound by The Amadeus Press Limited

More Memories of
of
Middlesbrough

Contents

Introduction

Children taking part in the
Corpus Christi parade in 1966.

'Sweet, sweet the memories you gave to me.' So sang Dean Martin in his famous hit recording of 1956. You are about to go back to that era and beyond on a tour of pure nostalgia for the days of the last century that are precious to all of us. They are the ones we grew up in, the years in which our parents and grandparents made their way through life. 'More Memories of Middlesbrough' is a brand new collection of photographs that will awaken half forgotten thoughts of yesteryear and confirm the stories and descriptions of life in the town that an older generation told us about. Carefully researched text, adding depth and interest, enhance each image. Sometimes the writing is factual, elsewhere it is wry. But, in every case, it gives the reader something to consider about life and times as they used to be. The aim of this book is not to provide a history lesson, but to allow the reader to wallow in nostalgia and even shed a tear or two for that which can never be revisited. The good old days were not always so, as there were those of sadness as well as joy. They

are recalled on the following pages, acting as a contrast to the many happy memories springing from the remainder. 'Memories are made of this', Dino used to warble, so share them with us as we take that trip back in time to a century that brought us motor cars, aeroplanes and electrical appliances. Come back to an age of iron, steel and shipyards. See again life in Middlesbrough County Borough before the County of Cleveland was so much as a twinkle in the politician's eye.

Before turning the first page and taking that initial step back in time it is worth considering how far the town has come in a relatively short period. Many British towns and cities can trace their heritage back to Norman, Saxon or Roman times. Some go even further than that. But Middlesbrough is almost unique in its development. Now the largest town in the Teesside area, it was but a tiny collection of two dozen people scratching a living on the south bank of the river at the beginning of the 19th century. The coming of the railway changed all that, Middlesbrough becoming the first town in

England to owe its existence to the goods and passenger transport system that helped revolutionise Victorian Britain. When, in 1821, George Stephenson heard of Edward and Joseph Pease's intention to build a rail link between Stockton and Darlington to exploit a rich vein of coal, he persuaded them to use steam engines rather than horse power. The first locomotives ran on the line in 1825 and, five years later, it was extended east of Stockton to where land had been acquired for the creation of a new coal exporting port. A group of businessmen, who became known as 'The Owners', had bought Middlesbrough Farm and developed it as the home for a new community. The first houses were built, marking the coming of Middlesbrough as a town and the population grew sixfold to 154 by 1831. If that rise in numbers seemed grand, then the 1841 census showed an almost miraculous increase. In just a decade the town was home to 5,463. Henry Bolckow and John Vaughan opened their Iron Works and would play major parts in the growth of the area as their industries provided employment for thousands. The Owners were instrumental in the opening of the docks to the east of the town in 1842 and the scene was set for the further boom years of the second half of the century. Huge deposits of iron ore were discovered at Eston Beacon and steel mills, factories and shipyards dominated the skyline. By the turn of the century 80,000 people called Middlesbrough their home. It was a far cry from the handful who did so when the century began.

But it is to the developments of the 20th century that we turn for 'More Memories of Middlesbrough'. The pictures from between the wars show how the town began to change from its reliance on heavy industry to a more mixed economy. There was a growth in investment in other commercial areas and housing initiatives changed the face of Middlesbrough from the grid iron pattern laid down in the 1850s. They were also times of change on the streets. Motor cars, electric trams and buses made their entrance and altered the way people travelled. For some they were very difficult days. The dark clouds of the depression years hung above families living on the bread line. Then came the second world war and with it more death and destruction. Within this book you will get a flavour of those years and how our parents won through, thanks to a mixture of

An expectant group of people pose outside the Mariners' Tavern in 1929, before setting off on a day trip.

determination and sacrifice. Then came the years of rebuilding. The town centre was revamped after the war and new housing programmes mushroomed, especially in east Middlesbrough. The economy took an upsurge in the late 1950s and 1960s, leading to further central developments as new indoor shopping centres made their appearance.

It is the changing face of Middlesbrough, allied to changing lifestyles, that the following pages will highlight. Some things are lost forever, but many can be brought back to mind by a simple memory jogger. Who can ever really forget the smell of freshly baked bread wafting across the pavement from the bakery? The sight of rabbits, chickens and haunches of beef hanging on hooks outside the butcher's and the rattle of the Morris Cowley lumbering along Linthorpe Road are not that far back in history. With the help of this book and just a little imagination they are back with us again. Forget about the traffic jams, the multi storey car parks and dreaded office blocks and shop again at Newhouses Corner. Pop into Binns' department store or while away a few hours enjoying the Pathè newsreel and 'Reach for the Sky' showing at the Gaumont. Draw out a few bob from the York and County

Savings Bank and blow it on a perm in the hairdressing salon at Dickenson and Benson's store. It is all possible, thanks to 'More Memories of Middlesbrough'. You are about to return to a land of tanners and half crowns, to a time when traders could weigh in pounds and ounces without being prosecuted and to the days of the dolly tub and mangle. Play board games with the children once more when they have tired of hopscotch, marbles, conkers and jacks. Pull up a chair and put another lump of coal on the fire. That should help rekindle the nostalgic mood. Reach for a glass of dandelion and burdock, filled from a stone jar, and pick up a Penny Arrow bar to chew on. Light up a Craven A, if you wish, and smooth down your sack dress or slick your hair back with Brilliantine. Wind up the gramophone, put a new needle into the stylus and let Nat 'King' Cole soothe you with 'Mona Lisa'. Older readers can toss a farthing to decide who can turn the first page. The lucky winner is about to begin a journey to a Middlesbrough that we should never forget. It is our heritage; something to be proud of as it helped make each and every one of us the people we are today.

Street scenes

The Captain Cook public house on Durham Street is within spitting distance of the Transporter Bridge, but its pedigree is much older. It opened in 1842 and is still serving ale today, even though the property all around it has long gone. As it is now a listed building of historical interest, long may it survive. The lovely ornamental gable work is a fine testament to the craftsmanship of the Victorian builder. Looking carefully at the Captain Cook in 1950, further evidence of careful artwork can be found displayed on the attractively patterned screens inside the ground floor windows. It is typical of the attention to detail given to a hotel of its era. The pub sign that swings over the front door today shows Captain Cook using a sextant. The museum in Stewart Park is dedicated to the memory of the exploits of this famous son of Marton. Born in 1728, this naval captain, navigator and explorer travelled the coasts and seaways of Canada before embarking on three Pacific expeditions in the 1770s. There he ranged from the Antarctic ice fields to the Bering Strait and from the coasts of North America to Australia and New Zealand. Polynesian natives in the Sandwich Islands (Hawaii) murdered him in 1779, but the new standards of thoroughness in discovery and seamanship that James Cook set ensure his privileged place in history.

Tyne Street, in the old town, connected Lower Feversham Street and Bridge Street East. These are the homes that our grandparents possibly grew up in, back to back terraces and, for some, a communal street tap as many houses did not have running water. There was not even a back yard to hang out the washing, so it was strung across the street. Housing conditions appear primitive to us today, cocooned in our centrally heated homes and aided by modern electrical appliances that make housework a doddle. Even in the 1950s washing machines, fridges and electric irons were luxury items, not the necessities they are today. The building at the far end of the street was an important entertainment centre, the Oxford Palace of Varieties. This music hall opened on 9 August 1867 and audiences were entertained by Alvante and Petro Athos on the flying trapeze, Kate Chatters and Tom Crosling, billed as 'a negro artist'. More famous names than those trod the boards in later years. Dan Leno, the first music hall artist to appear at a Royal Command Performance, starred here, Harry Houdini performed escapology, Harry Lauder sang and Charlie Chaplin performed routines to packed houses. In later life the Oxford Palace of Varieties became a warehouse and was used by the Diamond Grit works before falling victim to a bombing raid in 1940.

Right: It is sad that at times in the last century our parents had no sense of history, or they would not have allowed so many noble buildings to be demolished. They seemed to think that doing away with the old was a sign of modern thinking, so out went the baby and the bath water together. Some structures could not be classed as noble or grand, but they had a place in showing the development of Middlesbrough from a tiny hamlet to a town of major proportions. Yet, this was all swept away in the rush to prove that concrete, steel and glass, erected many storeys high, was what the public wanted. In truth, it did not really matter what it wanted; this was what it was going to get. All that remains of 28 West Street is a humble plaque to the memory of the first house to appear in the new town of Middlesbrough. George Clapham built it in 1830, but it was demolished in September 1959 without a care for the place it held in the town's heritage. Memories of Trainor's hairdressers and Robinson's general store that traded close by are almost gone forever. How better they could have been preserved if only our parents had stopped to think before swinging the demolition hammer.

Below: The billboard in the distance extolled the virtues of William Younger's famous beers, but the Talbot Hotel had ceased serving any brew at all by June 1958. Standing forlornly, a shadow of its former self, on the corner of South Street and the old market square, its days were numbered. Peeling paint, broken windows and a general air of neglect promised the inevitable. It was demolished shortly after this photograph was taken. It was sad to see the old buildings disappear as the country entered a period of prosperity. These were the 'never had it so good' years that Prime Minster Harold Macmillan reminded electors they were experiencing. Unemployment was falling, wages were rising and consumer goods that were once luxury items became commonplace. Car ownership was on the increase and Monday's washing was often spun dry rather than pegged out on the line. Another of Macmillan's memorable phrases, 'wind of change', could have been applied to the Talbot as it was swept away from the site it had occupied since 1844. Also known as 'the Dog' or 'Sacker's', the latter after an early landlord, Peter Sacker, the hotel's public bar used to be busy with men playing pub games that are a mystery to modern youth. Cribbage, don, solo and nap were some of the popular card games, all of which had their own mystique and unique language. Cries of 'one for his nob', 'ten for game' and 'misÉre' would make youngsters of today scratch their heads, but in the Talbot we knew what they meant.

All over the country town halls were festooned and garlanded in honour of King George VI and Queen Elizabeth. Hopefully they used stronger glue to hold in place the letters in the loyal message! Something seems to have come adrift, but we know that the sentiments stayed intact. It looks to have been a chilly May day in 1937 from the way in which the pedestrians are dressed. The men have their flat caps firmly pulled down and the woman, striding purposefully across the street in her sensible shoes, is warmly wrapped up in a heavy coat and fur collar. The pair sitting in the open fronted Fred Stonehouse van, on its way to Acklam Street, must have found it a draughty journey. The road for the new king was to be one that he felt he had been blown along. All his early life had been in the shadow of his popular, outgoing elder brother. He had been happy to play second fiddle, shunning the limelight. In a matter of months he found himself in the glare of the spotlight, leading to the day when he stood with his wife, Elizabeth, and children, Elizabeth and Margaret, on the balcony of Buckingham Palace. Nervously acknowledging the cheers of the crowd, he stood dressed in robes of deep red and snow white ermine, knowing that fate had dealt him a hand he was unsure how to play.

Top: West Street, in the old town, is one of the original streets of the grid iron laid out around the market square in 1830. The King William IV, fondly known as the 'King Billy', had been doing a roaring trade for well over a century when this scene was captured in March 1955. The pub first opened its doors in 1832, only two years after the first house was built. How many pints had been poured from jugs or pulled through the pipes from the cellar in the intervening years? The chap leaving the taproom would not be worried by such trivialities as he was happy to end his working day with a glass or two of Younger's beer. Beer in 1955 cost a matter of a shilling or so, not the two quid or more charged for a pint in some upmarket hostelries today. That amount would have made a huge hole in his wage packet back then, the average weekly wage being a lot less than a tenner. But, at least there was work to be had. The country was beginning to turn the corner after a decade of postwar austerity. Rationing had finished the previous year, sausages were plentiful at Hartley's and Mr Churchill was in control of the government. Everything on the horizon looked stable, but how quickly things can change. Within a month the inept Anthony Eden was prime minister, a woman was on trial for capital murder and civil war had broken out in the Far East. Eventually, Mr Eden would muddle through the Suez crisis, Ruth Ellis become the last woman in Britain to be hanged and the fragile world peace would be threatened by the Vietnam War.

Top right: The diversion around Park Road North was completed in October 1954 and this was part of the resultant scene on 17 November. The picture is dominated by the two structures that still hold pride of place here half a century on. Thousand upon thousand have gathered around the Cenotaph, laying wreaths and saying prayers, each year since it was dedicated on 11 November 1922.

The £11,000 Aberdeen granite memorial was unveiled by the deputy mayor, Councillor JG Pallister, accompanied by two blind war veterans whose presence heightened the sadness of the proceedings. The Cenotaph is close to the main entrance to Albert Park, where the Dorman Memorial Museum was built on the east side of Linthorpe Road at a cost of £15,000. It was handed over to the mayor, Councillor AC Dorman, by his father on 1 July 1904. Colonel J Hoole performed the official opening ceremony as the museum was dedicated to the memory of the mayor's brother, AL Dorman, a member of the Green Howards, killed in the Boer War. The Dorman Museum developed through the last century to the level at which it could boast that it had something for everyone. In 2001 major refurbishing and redevelopment prepared for the interests of a new millennium with activity areas, discovery zones, a pottery gallery and much more to interest locals and tourists alike.

Right: This was the heart of Middlesbrough, a century or more before this 1950s photograph was taken. It was the hub of the town's commerce, the site of a thriving weekly market and the very centre of all life. The square had all that newcomers wanted, a pub, a church, its administrative town hall and a place to buy and trade goods. The first streets and houses were laid out in regimented lines, in

grid iron fashion, away from the square. East Street, West Street, Suffield Street and Feversham Street are just a few of the names of the initial ones. They still survive, but are no longer fresh, new and full of hope for the future. The district has an air of abandonment hanging over it these days, despite the presence of a small housing estate nearby. The market, introduced by the 1841 Middlesbrough Improvement Act, closed in 1959. At around the same time, what had been the Wesleyan Chapel was pulled down. Built in 1838, on the far side of the market place, it had been used by the Guisborough Shirt Company as a factory since 1949. The church spire in the distance belongs to St Hilda's, then the parish church. The old Town Hall, to the right, opened in 1846, but became redundant as the main seat of local government when the new one was built in Victoria Square just over 40 years later. The old building is now a sad, lonely sight, a shell of its former glory.

Above: Sir Samuel Alexander Sadler (1842-1911), a former soldier and Middlesbrough MP, looks across Victoria Gardens from his statue towards the magistrates' court and, to the left, the police station. The law courts replaced the buildings of the former Hugh Bell School. The gardens, popular with office workers in the summer during lunch hour, were once the site of a cattle market and a venue for open air entertainment. Jugglers, acrobats, fire eaters and musicians made it a lively spot. Circuses were held here and it even boasted a skating rink in former times. Before he got onto his plinth, Colonel Sadler opened Victoria Square or Gardens in 1901. There is a corresponding statue, on the opposite side of gardens, looking back across at Sadler. It commemorates the contribution that John Vaughan (1799-1868) made to the town's formative years. Born in Worcester, he travelled to earn his living in Cumbria and on Tyneside. Vaughan teamed up with Henry Bolckow in Middlesbrough operating an iron making firm, bringing the ore into town and then out by rail to the blast furnaces at Witton Park, County Durham. Having been transformed into pig iron, it was returned to the Middlesbrough foundry. The longwinded process was short circuited when, in 1850, Vaughan found large ironstone deposits in the Cleveland Hills at Eston. Rail links were quickly established between his quarry and the ironworks in town. Industrial Middlesbrough was on its way towards the boom years.

Body and soul come together in this picture, taken on 9 April 1962. The church provided an opportunity for meditation, the pub gave relaxation and the bridge transportation. St Hilda's Parish Church was built with seating for 600 worshippers and a service of consecration held in 1840. The addition of a new gallery in 1861 offered places for another 300 to give thanks to God and those who had given so generously towards its building costs. These had been raised by public subscription, with the land being freely given by Joseph Pease and 'The Owners' of the Middlesbrough Estate. By the date of this scene, St Hilda's was struggling to continue its life as a vibrant parish church. The vicar left and no replacement could be found. The population had moved away to newer areas, so the congregation dwindled. The clergy at All Saints, Linthorpe Road, took over the running of St Hilda's until its demolition in 1970. In the distance, on North Street, the man and van are outside the Middlesbrough Hotel. Built on the site of an ancient Benedictine priory, it had been a popular watering hole since 1846. Landlords used to joke that it was more of a holy watering hole, because of its religious connections! The Middlesbrough Hotel was a handy stopping off place for those en route to or from the Transporter Bridge, seen behind and above North Street.

Albert Road, on 16 July 1969, was about to undergo a major face lift. The Corporation Hotel, on the corner of Corporation Road, and this stretch of Albert Road disappeared under the developments that became Corporation House and the Cleveland Centre. Lauriston's solicitor's office, the Hunting travel agent and Patricia's hairstyling salon would all have to find new homes. A mini skirted blonde passing in front of Permanent House could have commented that the building would not live up to its name. The young woman's dress sense was typical of the time, legs either being

bared or covered in thigh length boots. There seemed to be no in between. Foreign cars did not dominate the roads as they do today, so the Mk 1 Ford Cortina coming towards the camera is a good reminder that once Britain was a major player in motor manufacturing. The man sweeping the pavement outside

Patricia's might have noticed a subtle shift in the descriptions given to such businesses. They were no longer hairdressers, but stylists, taking their shops, sorry salons, into a new art form. The word 'unisex' was not far behind, much to the horror of some old stagers.

Top: Motoring restrictions came thick and fast in the 1970s, making life hard for the car driver. No parking areas even became no go areas as yellow became the predominant colour in the town. It was daubed on kerbs and in the gutters, even appearing in the middle of the road in the form of grids that a car was forbidden to enter until an exit was clear. Motorists felt as though they were being squeezed out, but they were not the only ones to suffer. It was ironic that the building of new ring roads around the town could only be achieved by sacrificing some of Middlesbrough's historic buildings. Instead of protecting them from the motor car in the town centre, the flyover and bypass were the cause of their destruction. The Royal Exchange had held an imposing position on the corner of Albert Road and Marton Road since its opening on 29 July 1868. Built at a cost of over £30,000 to replace the former exchange that had only existed for 30 years, the Royal Exchange included shops and dining facilities within its walls, in addition to the exchange room. When it was demolished in 1985, as part of the improvements for the A66 flyover, Middlesbrough lost more than a building where people traded iron, steel and other commodities. A little piece of its soul went with it.

Above: The Corporation Hotel dominated the corner of the junction with Albert Road where Corporation House now stands. The 272 bus to Billingham was packed with passengers as it travelled bumper to bumper with the car in front and the other bus behind. In the late 1960s traffic flow was becoming a major headache and moves were afoot to get

some of the traffic off the streets. Parking restrictions were already in force, helped by the ever vigilant 'meter maid', seen on the left, satchel full of tickets and pen in hand, ready to pounce. Eventually, pedestrianised zones and bus only lanes would be introduced to make town centre shopping and access a safer and more pleasant experience. They also helped to make the motorist feel like a leper, an unwanted guest at the ball. The 1960s were not only the years of change for road users, they also saw a shift in lifestyle. Children born in the baby boomer years after the war reached adulthood. They had come into a world that had promised them greater freedom and they demanded its delivery. Young people rebelled against some of the values of their parents and 'did their own thing'. They wanted wine bars and clubs, not old hotels. The Corporation Hotel, built in 1905 to replace an earlier building used as licensed premises since 1863, became a relic of the past. It was demolished in 1971.

Events & occasions

Even flat caps change in style as the years go by. The ones on display outside Marton Hall were a wide variety that threatened to cast the wearers into a life of permanent shade. Their owners came to the Hall on 25 May 1928 to participate in the official opening of Stewart Park. Marton Hall was once the home of Henry Bolckow, Middlesbrough's first MP, who had it built for him in 1853 near the site of the former Marton Lodge that had burned down in 1832. Although still owned by the Bolckow family, the Hall lay empty for many years in the early 20th century until it was used as a military training base in World War I. After the war the Council decided to acquire the house and estate for public use, but it took until 1923 to reach agreement with the Bolckows. It was agreed to pay £35,000 for 210 acres of farmland, but the coffers were looking empty when the Council turned its attention to buying the Hall and the remainder of the parkland. Councillor Thomas D Stewart, mayor in 1920, stepped into the breach with a generous offer. He provided £25,000 from his own pocket to close the deal, the park being named after him in way of thanks. When Marton Hall burned down in 1960 its fine Italian marble interior architecture was lost in addition to a little piece of history.

Right: Mayor Alderman Kedward, resplendent in his fine robes of office and mayoral chain, led the way into church on 11 November 1929 for the annual remembrance service. Flanked by veterans of the first world war, he was attending that special thanksgiving to the memory of all those who gave their lives in the service of their country, a scene repeated every year even now. Sadly, such is the nature of the beast, man still cannot resolve his differences with others without resorting to the bullet and the bomb. When Mayor Kedward lifted his voice in the hymn 'For those in peril' he must have thought that the sacrifices made in the mud of Flanders and the shell holes on the Somme would ensure that, never again, would the world see such carnage. The government had promised those lucky enough to come back from the front that they would have a land fit for heroes in which to live. That was still some way off as Britain struggled against the tide of the depression years. Wages were low and unemployment high, but for one Sunday in November we were all on the same level. Everyone remembered a loved one who never came back, a neighbour who was no more. We bowed our heads and said 'Lest we forget'.

Bottom: When Mayoress Mrs Kedward collected the bouquets and posies presented to her by the children she probably did not realise that she was helping the sun set on the British Empire. In 1930 we still had a map of the world that had huge chunks coloured in pink. Although we celebrated Empire Day, the world order was changing. After World War One, when we had declared war on Germany for the whole of the British Empire, the dominions signed the peace treaty and joined the League of Nations as separate countries. Mahatma Ghandi, the Indian activist, had for years been demanding that his country gain full independence. Others shared his beliefs for their homelands. In 1931 the Statute of Westminster recognised that a British Commonwealth of Nations existed, comprising of different independent countries. That only partly satisfied many and they continued to press for greater autonomy and full independence after World War II. India, Pakistan, Ceylon (Sri Lanka) and Burma (Myanmar) broke free in the late 1940s. All this lay ahead for Mrs Kedward and the children pressing their gifts upon her. How stylish she looked in the wide brimmed hat and fur stole, but imagine how derided she would be by animal lovers today. Next to her stood a young woman of the modern era, showing an attractive amount of leg and daringly hatless as well. Two years earlier women had gained full equality in the polling booths and she was going to display her own independent streak, in addition to her calves.

Below: Ayresome Park has seen some crowds in its time. The terraces have been crammed, the crush bars threatening to buckle under the strain, as Wilf Mannion's skills lit up the play or Brian Clough arrogantly slotted in his five goals against Brighton in 1958. The roar of the crowd on those days was of a deeper tone than the decibel crunching screech from 20,000 children on 2 July 1930. They waved their flags and gave the adults with them severe headaches that took hours to recover from. There was good reason to be excited, the Prince of Wales was visiting. This was a time long before television, so the opportunity to see even images of royalty was limited. There were glimpses in cinema newsreels and photographs in newspapers, but the Royal Family was still sufficiently remote to be placed on an adoring pedestal. Little wonder that we went into a frenzy when there was the chance to see a royal in the flesh. In that between the wars era the monarchy was very popular, but the nation's affection and loyalty was to be sorely tested a few years later. When, in 1936, the Prince of Wales succeeded his father to the throne as Edward VIII his short reign was blighted by scandal. His involvement with the twice divorced American socialite, Wallis Simpson, split the country. Failing to win government and church support, he abdicated. Some of those who cheered him at Ayresome Park also jeered him off into exile.

They hung out of windows, climbed lampposts, sat on the rooftops or merely struggled on the pavement to get a better view. The cause of all the excitement was not the Middlesbrough soccer team bringing home the FA Cup, now that would be a novelty, nor some boy band passing through on the way to a concert hall full of teeny boppers. Both of those events might provoke such a scene of wild passions, but look at the hats the women are wearing and the style of uniform sported by the police. These are the fashions of over 70 years ago. It was 2 July 1930 and the focus of attention was the Prince of Wales.

The heir to the throne, or Prince Edward Albert Christian George Andrew Patrick David to give him his full title, came to town to open the new technical school, Constantine College. The 35 year old king in waiting was hugely popular as the country's most eligible bachelor. Women swooned at his picture, but to see him in real life was more than some could bear. They pushed and shoved with all their might to get a better sight of the handsome prince. Mounted police knew how to control football crowds and lines of striking workers, but screaming women were something else. 'Please, sergeant, can you send me to a nice, simple riot next time?'

Above: The rain did not dampen the high spirits of the crowd outside Middlesbrough Town Hall as it celebrated the coronation of a new king. A grand statue of George VI was framed in the entrance, underneath garlands of flowers, crowns and streamers that decorated the length and breadth of the building. Many of the flags and much of the bunting had been in use two years before when we celebrated George V's jubilee. We had thought that it would be in use again for the coronation of Edward VIII, but his abdication put things on hold. As the old king had

died on 20 January 1936 the nation waited 16 months until a new one could be crowned. The former Prince of Wales had departed into history before he could receive the crown in Westminster Abbey, so it was not until 12 May 1937 that Britain could officially mark the ceremonial day. Policemen, their capes buttoned down against the rain, joined in the three cheers given for their Majesties, though they stopped short at throwing their helmets in the air. The rest of the crowd was less inhibited. There was dancing in the gardens, laughter in the square and partying in the streets. Some of the joy was relief that the monarchy could return to normal after the abdication crisis six months earlier.

Top: Happy smiles adorned the faces of the pretty girls looking forward to participating in the Middlesbrough Pageant, one of the best loved traditions in the town. In those worrying days leading up to the war it was fun to forget the rumblings of the Fascists on the Continent and allow ourselves the joys of taking part in traditional merrymaking. St Paul's Church, Newport Road, had stood in the densely populated Cannon Street area since 1871. These children posed outside it on the back of a lorry gaily decorated to act as a float for this jolly day in May 1937. The gardener watering her 'flowers' played the part of Mary in a representation of the nursery rhyme 'Mary, Mary, quite contrary'. Mums and dads watched proudly from the pavement as the tableau passed by to the oohs and aahs of so many doting parents. How innocent the looks on those angelic faces, how much happiness they brought to all who knew them. By now these lovely lasses will be in their 70s, but what happy memories they must have of the day they bloomed under the spray from Mary's watering can. The same cannot be said of the church as it withered and died. Failing to make its centenary, it was demolished in 1967.

Right: More tea, vicar, or would you prefer something stronger after the donkey derby? Poole Sanatorium, once the home of an industrialist, was a refuge for those stricken by illness. It opened its grounds to Councillor Cooper, Reverend Smith, Alderman Marshall and others as part of the celebrations being held to honour the jubilee of King George V. The 'sailor king' was popular with the masses for his blunt, no nonsense approach. He told it as he saw it and was loved for doing so. Once asked what he thought about foreign travel, he responded, 'Abroad? Been there once, didn't like it.' On 6 May 1935 this fun loving trio of jockeys was the envy of the lads standing behind them. How they would have loved to replace them on the donkeys' backs. The boys would have brought their riding skills to bear, honed as they were from donkey rides on the sands at Saltburn and Redcar. But they would have to wait their turn, for the big boys were enjoying themselves too much. It must be something about the male genes that makes men continue to look for opportunities to relive their childhood, as if they have never really grown up. Why else do they stop in front of toyshop windows, gazing longingly at Dinky cars? Now you know why they refused to dismount and let someone else have a turn.

Bottom: These are some of the prize winners from a Pageant fancy dress parade. The problem with such competitions is that there are so many losers. Only those who have been put into a situation like that can appreciate the disappointment children feel when they are overlooked. They have spent all morning putting on make up, adjusting their costumes and being told by their mums that they are bound to do well. Then comes the moment when some bigwig taps the person next to you on the shoulder and you know it is not your day. It is scant consolation for your mother to tell you that to her you will always be number one. Anyway, what do the judges know about anything? They take no notice of originality, always choosing a contestant who has relied more on mum's sewing ability or a specially hired costume than his own ingenuity. The lad in the middle won first prize, but it seems hard to understand what set him apart from the rest. The second prize winner would be disqualified these days on the grounds of racial stereotyping. No one in the group seems to have enjoyed the competition, but perhaps the photographer caught them on an off moment.

Above: When we remember those who made the ultimate sacrifice in defence of our realm it makes no difference where or when it was they fell. The price they paid is just the same. It is recalled every year at memorials, cenotaphs and in services in villages, towns and cities across the country. Each Remembrance Sunday is not just an opportunity to give homage to those who went before, but to say thanks to those who survived. On 13 November 1949 veterans of different campaigns came together to express mutual admiration. The two grand old men proudly displaying their service medals had marched off to war when Victoria was on the throne, 50 years before this picture was taken. They had been in South Africa, fighting the Boer War, a conflict that became an embarrassment in our military history. Inspired by the richness of the diamond fields, Britain claimed the rights of an overlord to these deposits in the Transvaal. The war of 1899-1902 followed, leaving Britain with egg on its face as it struggled to subdue guerilla fighters with its crack troops. That should not have taken away the glory due to these old soldiers who risked their lives in service of the Queen. Let us not forget, either, that the young ATS woman admiring their medals was herself a veteran, a volunteer in support of her King and country.

Bottom: You would have thought there would have been a better turn out to help celebrate the centenary of the day when Middlesbrough received its charter of incorporation. Perhaps this was just a slack period as the display in the Municipal Art Gallery was open from 10 January to 4 February 1953. There was quite a lot of information to take in as visitors looked around the gallery walls. Photographs of buses, libraries, schools, hospitals and parkland reminded residents of some of the services the Council provided. Above them the important events of previous years were flagged up, reminding us that the new gas holder in Cannon Park was completed in 1926, the first branch library came to North Ormesby the following year and the Little Theatre presented its first production in 1930. Facts and figures adorned other parts of the display area, listing the meteoric rise in population since Henry Bolckow became the first mayor in 1853. He was an immigrant from Mecklenberg in northeast Germany who had found work in Newcastle in 1824. Moving to Middlesbrough in 1841, he joined forces with John Vaughan to sink their savings into iron making. Bolckow went on to become the first president of the Chamber of Commerce, being further honoured in 1868 as the town's first MP.

Above: The workers were on the march along Albert Road in the mid 1960s, expressing an unhappiness with pay and conditions that led to a number of scenes of unrest for the government to tackle. The decade began with the Tories in control, led by Harold Macmillan, a prime minister who had such public and press support that he revelled in the nickname 'Supermac'. Attitudes changed when he stepped down through ill health in October 1963, being replaced by the aristocratic Alec Douglas-Home. This ineffectual leader lacked the common touch and only lasted a year in power, narrowly losing the 1964 general election to Harold Wilson's Labour Party. The new government held a firmer grip on power when another general election, 18 months later, gave Wilson a large majority. His troubles were only just beginning as clashes with the unions over incomes restraint. The wages freeze fuelled strikes by seamen and car workers in 1966, bringing trades unionists onto the streets in marches of solidarity. It was a time of protest on the hoof as anti Vietnam War protestors marched and ban the bomb CND followers descended on Aldermaston. In 1970 Harold Wilson tried to regain popular support, surrendering to union demands for large pay increases, but the public had become tired of strife and gave its vote to Ted Heath to try his luck.

Below: Corpus Christi is an important feast day in the church calendar, especially honoured by the Catholic Church. Literally translated as 'body of Christ' the festival is a special commemoration of the communion host, the procession being the only occasion when the Eucharist is paraded in public. This procession along Albert Road took place on the Sunday immediately following Corpus Christi, from its inception by Bishop Lacy in 1925 until 1971. Apart from one cancellation during the war, the event attracted thousands onto the streets every year to watch the parade go by. It took an age for the whole stream to go past. A police car led the way, followed by the Cathedral band, a cross bearer, scouts, schoolchildren from St Mary's, St Philomena's, St Mary's and others, Young Christian Workers, altar boys, priests, nuns and the faithful. Another band and police car brought up the rear, giving the procession a form of symmetry. These devout children displayed their hearts and their beliefs on their sleeves in 1966. Even in the swinging 60s there was time to think of higher things than the Beatles and Mary Quant. Those were the days of Whit walks, when we got new clothes and visited relatives we had not seen since last year, hopeful of a top up to our money boxes.

Right: All the nice girls love a sailor, plus some of the naughty ones too! In July 1966 HMS Tiger arrived and held an open day for the general public to look around this famous cruiser. In the foreground, as viewed from the bridge, are the barrels of its forward twin three inch automatic anti aircraft turret. Beyond is the mounting for twin six inch automatic anti surface guns. Weighing some 12,000 tons, the 'Tiger' was previously named HMS Bellerophon, but was upgraded by the Royal Navy in 1965 to become one of Britain's three missile guided cruisers. Its name will live on in history because of its involvement in Rhodesia's unilateral declaration of independence. After her visit to Middlesbrough, she set off on patrol in the Mediterranean. There, in December, she received a message ordering her to the British port and colony of Gibraltar. The crew was not informed of the situation and, on arrival, eyebrows were raised when officials boarded the ship. To the surprise of the ratings they turned out to be none other than our prime minister, Harold Wilson, and Ian Smith, the Rhodesian leader. The discussions between the two politicians became known as the 'Tiger Talks'. At the time the 'Tiger' was one of the deadliest cruisers Britain has ever seen, backing up its firepower with four Wessex Sea King helicopters. Despite that, it never saw true combat and was taken out of service in 1978, being scrapped in the 1980s.

Bottom: Left hand down a bit, to you, to me, pushing and shoving with all their might, council workmen and Territorial Army personnel combined forces on this manoeuvre. The gun was a relic of the Battle of Sebastopol, one of the epic events of the Crimean War. This important naval base was vital to the Russian Black Sea fleet in the war against Britain and France. From 17 October 1854 to 11 September 1855 a huge force of 50,000 troops, jointly commanded by Lord Raglan and General Canrobert, besieged and finally captured the city. The gun was a trophy acquired by the council in 1857. Too large to fit on a mantelpiece in the Town Hall, it was sited near St Hilda's Church. In later years it was moved to a prominent position in Albert Park, before going on its travels once more, arriving in Stewart Park c1950. On 21 May 1965 the Territorials took it under their wing, moving the gun to their headquarters on Stockton Road. There were big guns firing elsewhere in the world that year, none more important than those being shot by the Americans as they entered the Vietnam War. At home, a single bullet was enough to put paid to the life of our former world light heavyweight boxing champion. In the small hours of the morning of 24 July, Freddie Mills was found in a car in Soho, dying from a head wound.

Wartime

liens have landed, watch out, take over! Strange looking beings, recognisable by their long snouts, have invaded from a distant planet and taken over Brambles Infant School. This is 1938 and such a story is completely credible, just ask America. There Orson Welles has recently broadcast a radio play, based on the HG Wells' novel 'War of the Worlds'. So realistic was the adaptation that thousands believed they were listening to a newscast, panicked and ran screaming into the streets away from the invading Martians. But the British are not gullible, unlike our counterparts across the pond. We immediately recognise this as a civil defence exercise at the

school. During the Great War many soldiers suffered horribly, on both sides, from the effects of mustard and chlorine gas used as a weapon at the front. Memories of those horrors came back to mind as the world lurched towards another major conflict, fuelling fears that aircraft could release gas bombs on innocent citizens. In Middlesbrough over 100,000 masks were issued. Civil defence groups, such as the WVS, organised practice sessions to teach civilians what to do if under attack. These infants, sitting on their camp beds, might have thought it was a game to dress up like this. Thankfully, the gas masks were never needed, but it was only right to have been ready, just in case.

When the bombs fall from the sky they do not distinguish between industrial and private property, nor do they worry about whether it is your house or that of God. St Peter's Church, only the second Anglican church to be erected 'over the border', had served its parish with distinction since its consecration on 2 September 1873. Built of plain brick in the English style, it acquired a more distinctive look in 1901 when the tower and spire, donated by Sir Raylton and Lady Dixon, were added. Although those additions were only partially damaged in one of the air raids in June 1940, the body of the church was completely wrecked. Parishioners stood around the shell on the following morning, scarcely able to believe their eyes at the sacrilege committed by Goering's pilots. Similar sentiments were expressed when Coventry's cathedral was destroyed five months later, a forerunner to the German Baedeker raids on cultural and historical targets. For two years after the raid on St Peter's, services were held in the church hall until the congregation transferred to St Hilda's. This was a coincidence, the two parishes having already combined in 1932. A new St Peter's Church Hall was put up at Thorntree, but vandalism badly affected it and the site was cleared in the late 1970s.

worked tirelessly in the war effort and who were ready to fight to the last, if need be. The King and Queen had won the admiration of their subjects by keeping London as their home, taking their chances with the rest of us when others might have been tempted to slink off to the country or overseas. George VI did not slip easily into this sort of role when he had to mingle with people. He was a shy and diffident man, but contrast that approach to the one displayed by his wife. She chatted happily to the volunteers with a relaxed air. In later years she became revered as the centenarian royal, our 'Queen Mum'. God bless you, ma'am.

Left: It is a forlorn scene of shattered hopes and dreams as well as shattered windows and smashed slates. A young boy wanders disconsolately from the scene as a postman on the corner wonders what to do with his delivery for 178 to 170 Marsh Road. The piles of sandbags on the right were no defence against the hail of death that fell from the sky on the night of 26 June 1940. There had been an earlier air raid that month and another in May, when the industrial area on the South Bank was targeted. Those attacks had caused little damage, but the residents of Marsh Road felt the full brunt of the latest strike. This was the beginning of a year long, almost nightly, assault on Britain's towns and industries that became known as 'the Blitz'. London suffered the

Bottom left: In 1941 war was raging on several fronts as we stood alone against the might of the Axis powers. Our troops battled with Rommel's Afrika Korps, we were driven out of Greece and our cities were under onslaught from the Luftwaffe's bombers. Our civil defences were well mobilised in case Hitler decided to invade, for he had threatened to do so the previous year, until the RAF was victorious in the Battle of Britain. King George VI and Queen Elizabeth went on a tour of the country to show their support for the Home Guard, Women's Voluntary Service, St John Ambulance, Red Cross and all the other bodies who

greatest casualties, but all over the country railway sidings, dockyards, factories and residential areas felt the pain and terror of the war. There was a spirit of defiance and togetherness about the British that saw us through, but do not imagine we smiled as the bombs fell and our homes were gutted. Some had nightmares for years afterwards, others did not survive to tell the tale. The enemy had decided that attacking 'soft' targets would bring the country to its knees, intending to provoke an anti government reaction to the horror of war. It miscalculated because the losses we suffered made us more determined than ever to fight back.

Below: Do not be fooled into thinking that this is a delightful rustic scene from the rural heartlands on the slopes of the Cleveland Hills. It is an image of wartime preparations taking place at 11 Eastbourne Road, Linthorpe, not much more than a mile from Middlesbrough town centre. The little girl is pumping out her private air raid shelter, that dug out covered by curved sections of corrugated iron that appeared in many gardens leading up to and in the early years of the second world war. This type of defence became known as the Anderson shelter, named after the Home Secretary of the day. Photographed in 1939, the girl's family was one of those who had taken the question of civil defence very seriously. In the late 1930s the country had been divided into two camps. There were those who believed in the success of peace overtures to Germany made by the prime minister, Neville Chamberlain, and those who listened to the warnings issued by the likes of Winston Churchill that Hitler was not to be trusted. When Chamberlain returned from Munich in 1938, waving his pathetic piece of paper that promised 'Peace in our time', many breathed a sigh of relief. The rest took a more realistic view, dug shelters, practised gas mask drill and waited for the balloon to go up.

On Remembrance Sunday uniformed men and women attended church services in memory of those who fell in the war. That was a sombre occasion when prayers were said, hymns were sung and the faces of lost comrades came back to mind. Later that week the British Legion held a festival of remembrance in the town hall, partly in recognition of the dead, but also as a celebration of what had been achieved. There was a time to mourn, but also one to rejoice. Sketches were performed and songs sung, bringing back images of ENSA entertainment parties and Vera Lynn dreaming of a time when little Jimmy could go to sleep in his own little room again. The lads adopted roles as wags, showing off in front of the girls. They responded as young women did the world over, giving a coy smile and a welcoming look. These men were their own version of the Crazy Gang, that bunch of wacky comics who included the inimitable 'Monsewer' Eddie Gray. They tried to impress girls who had grown up quickly during the war years. They had guided pilots on missions, plotted the track of enemy subs on sorties against our shipping and liaised with undercover agents abroad. These girls had ducked as their airfields were strafed and helped rescue the maimed from dockyards under bombardment. It would take more than a quick quip to win their hearts, for little girls had very quickly become knowing women.

Constant to the Constantine vision

How many readers have fond memories of evening classes or daytime courses at what is now the University of Teesside? This educational institution based on a single site in the centre of Middlesbrough has been serving the needs of local residents and of local industry for over seventy years. During that time it has undergone a number of name changes, as well as changes to the type of course it offers, but the University is fulfilling the same purpose the College has fulfilled throughout its history.

Although the need to create an institution in Middlesbrough to provide advanced education in technical and commercial subjects had been recognised in the late 1800s, the origins of the University of Teesside lie in the vision and extreme generosity of a local shipping magnate, Joseph Constantine. His attitude is well illustrated in part of the speech he made to the education committee in 1916: 'I have been identified with Middlesbrough the whole of my commercial life, and I have always felt that I should like to do something that might be of benefit to the community...We have been moving in very serious times lately, and it appears to all that when the time of peace comes we must be properly equipped to stand up against the very serious competition we must expect from other countries, including Germany.' The committee had no hesitation in accepting with gratitude the generosity of their benefactor.

Between 1916 and the formal opening of the college named after him by the then Prince of Wales in July 1930 Constantine donated over £80,000 to the enterprise.

This was an astronomical sum at the

Above left: Joseph Constantine. Above: A collection of Constantine College Brochures from the 1930s and 1950s.
Below: The original Constantine Building, 1930.

time and it made the building of the technical college in what is now the Constantine Building of the University on the junction of Borough Road and Albert Road possible.

From then until the late 1960s Constantine College provided a mix of further and higher education technical and commercial courses. Despite the economic difficulties of the time the College grew steadily with about 2,000, mainly part-time evening, students attending by the outbreak of the second world war.

The war inevitably saw a drop in the number of its students but Constantine College still provided vital training and educational services to the essential war industries of the region. One vital function was provision of technical training for the many women who came into local industries to replace the men conscripted into the armed forces.
The College even engaged in the

This page: *The opening of Constantine College by the then Prince of Wales, July 1930.*

production of specialist equipment for local firms during the war.

In the early post-war years, the College, which was already being overwhelmed by the growth of numbers before the outbreak of war, found itself in some difficulty to meet the great expansion in educational demands. With virtually no investment in buildings or equipment during the war the College struggled to accommodate the rising demand for places on its courses, especially with the growth of day release of young workers for educational purposes. What many before the war had seen as primarily an evening class centre became mainly a day college as the number of full-time students also increased. At the same time the number of students on full-time and

This page: *The Waterhouse Building.*

sandwich externally validated degree courses in subjects such as engineering, metallurgy and chemistry expanded and shifted the balance between further and higher education.

This shift led in the mid 1950s to a belief that the college should gain recognition as a College of Advanced Technology, one of eight that the government were planning to create. This attempt to boost the status of the College was ultimately unsuccessful, but it signalled a desire by the College and its controlling local education authority that it should become the basis of a fully-fledged institution of higher education.

By 1960 there were over five and a half thousand students, many still attending part-time evening classes. However, the crisis in accommodation had only been tackled by the construction of temporary buildings and by making use of secondary school premises and equipment in the evenings. During the 1960s the College offered seventeen degree

courses under the auspices of the new validating authority the Council for National Academic Awards. The narrow technical and commercial orientation of the College was broadened to include Liberal Studies in the humanities and social sciences.

After the creation of the unified Teesside local authority there developed a campaign for the creation of a university in the area and most importantly as far as Constantine College was concerned its designation as a polytechnic. This development meant that degrees with a strongly vocational character could be offered.

Above: *The Learning Resource Centre (opened in 1997) provides students with a full range of top quality facilities to support their studies. Being one of the best of its kind in the university sector students are able to use a full range of information sources from books to the web.*

It was about this time that the chronic shortage of suitable accommodation was addressed; the old High School buildings had been acquired and the highly visible eleven-storey tower block built.

In 1970, Constantine College was formally redesignated Teesside Polytechnic and its status as an institution of higher education clarified, though many locally still referred to it as Constantine College. The creation of the Polytechnic led to the development of plans for a huge expansion of the site and increased student numbers. These plans were, however, dogged by rather difficult relations with the local authorities, now split between the district of Middlesbrough responsible for planning, and the county of Cleveland the controlling education authority. There was also a current of feeling in some local political circles that the Polytechnic stood in the way of the creation of a university on Teesside.

By the late 1970s, Teesside Polytechnic had expanded but rather more modestly than had originally been envisaged.

In line with government policy, which was to sever links between the local education authorities and the polytechnics, Teesside gained independent corporate status in 1989. Middlesbrough then at long last became a university town in 1992 when the polytechnic became the University of Teesside. The campus also changed dramatically from that time with the building of new halls of residence, an award-winning Learning Resource Centre and most recently a new School of Health building. In fact, health is now the largest of the six schools in the University.

Above: *The Clarendon Building after its £5 million refurbishment in 1999.*

Technology remains important with over 1,600 students on science and applied technology courses, but even more are involved in computing and other information technology courses, undertaking studies beyond the imagination of the founders of Constantine College in 1930. Now, students at Teesside can study virtual reality, physiotherapy, sport and exercise, media studies, forensic science, law, graphic design, public relations or local medieval history to name just a very few of the undergraduate and postgraduate, full and part-time programmes now available at the University.

A major employer in its own right, and seen by government and the regional development agency as pivotal in the economic regeneration of the Tees Valley area, the founders of Constantine College would undoubtedly be proud that their creation had, almost three quarters of a century later, become an institution of 17,000 students equipped to meet the educational and professional development needs of the people of Teesside in a way appropriate to the changing industrial and economic climate.

*Top: The Centuria Building (opened in 2000) houses the School of Health, a 21st century state-of-the-art centre for the fast growing academic area on Teesside. **Above:** The Vice-Chancellor of the University of Teesside, Professor Derek Fraser. **Left:** The Innovation and Virtual Reality Centre, also home to the School of Science & Technology.*

At leisure

In 1929 JT Oliver was the licensee of the tavern that had first slaked the thirst of drinkers on Stockton Street in 1836. The party standing outside the Mariners' Tavern was mainly made up of women off on a day trip on a 'chara'. Most had put on their best hats for the occasion, though a few of the younger ones defied convention and went bareheaded. They could have been off to the seaside for their trip, perhaps as far down the coast as Whitby or Robin Hood's Bay. That would have been more of an adventure than just going to Saltburn-by-the-Sea. If they were headed inland, a real treat would have been to make an expedition to Harrogate. There the women could explore the lovely shops, pamper themselves in the refreshing spa waters at the Royal Baths and meet up at Betty's Tea Rooms to round off a wonderful day. Wherever they went, they sang 'One man went to mow' on the outward journey and nodded peacefully on the way back. There was no need for the crates of ale men seemed unable to do without on their day trips. They awoke just in time for a chorus of 'For he's a jolly good fellow' in honour of the driver, before popping some loose change into his hat and disappearing off back home to tell hubby of the delightful time they had.

Above: To the left, Miller's footwear shop was holding a clearance sale. It could have included some of the fixtures and fittings from the Grand Opera House, as the magnificent theatre was soon to put on its last presentation, 'Passion's Pleasures', prior to its closure on 21 June 1930. The opening production, on 7 December 1903, had been 'My Lady Mollie', but that was soon taken off and replaced by 'Aladdin', in time for its first pantomime season. Harry Tate, the popular impersonator, was the star who packed them in that Christmas. The Grand Opera House was built on land known as Swatters Carr, a site used in Victorian times by fairs and as a showground. To the right, theatregoers bought chocolate and tobacco from Williamson's to add to the enjoyment of witnessing the theatrical greats, like the Irvings and the Terrys. Opera companies provided highbrow entertainment as this corner of Southfield Road and Linthorpe Road dripped with culture. As tastes changed, locals turned their attention to the new rage, the talking picture movie. The theatre was remodelled and a projection room, screen and a magnificent Compton organ were installed. Renamed the Gaumont, the first reels were shown in the new cinema on 31 March 1931. When bingo and television drove the final nail in the coffin of going to the movies, it was appropriate that the last film to be shown on 29 February 1964 was called 'The Longest Day'.

Below: The winter of 1943 brought one of the turning points of the war. Hitler's ambitions to extend the influence of the third Reich, taking on the Russians in the east, cost Germany dear. His forces were overstretched, fighting on several fronts, and the harsh winter and stubborn resistance of the Red Army caused the Sixth Army to grind to a halt at Stalingrad. Surrounded by the Russians, cut off from supplies and reinforcements, estimates suggest that 200,000 German soldiers perished as much from cold and starvation as from the fighting. On 31 January 1943 Field Marshal von Paulus surrendered. Rita and Norman knew nothing of a Russian winter. They were just happy enjoying themselves in the snow on Manor Avenue, Linthorpe, taking turns pulling each other along on the little toboggan dad had knocked up in the garden shed. Perhaps that was he, keeping a watchful eye on this jolly pair of scamps through the front window. Elsewhere, other children used tin trays to slide down snowy slopes, threw snowballs at each other or built giant snowmen in the garden. Little pieces of coal for the eyes, a carrot as a nose, grandpa's pipe in his mouth and Frosty looked quite lifelike. Then came the thaw and the snows melted away, just like the Nazi dream of global conquest.

Below: The Central Library opened on 8 May 1912. Andrew Carnegie, the Scottish-American industrialist and philanthropist, had donated £15,000 to the cost of the building. The final bill reached £16,423, the shortfall being made up by public subscription and a further gift from Carnegie. His steel industries had made him fabulously rich. When he retired, in 1901, he turned his attention to diverting a lot of his time and money into helping develop the minds of his fellow human beings. Carnegie set up charitable trusts, including a major one for Scottish universities. All told he gave away £250 million. The same thoughts of helping the less fortunate were in the minds of the library staff as Christmas 1945 drew nearer. Though they could not afford to give millions, they could use their time and expertise in toy making. Needles flew and thimbles clicked as rag gollies, jolly bunnies and brightly painted dollies' faces appeared. Stored on spare bookshelves, they were awaiting transportation to local hospitals where they would find their way inside the stockings of the unlucky children spending the festive season in a hospital bed. The library staff was happy to help, having spent the war years jealously guarding every scrap of material that could go towards making a parachute or some other use as part of the war effort. It was a treat to be now able to use needlecraft skills and bring a smile to the faces of little kiddies who needed a lift.

Above: In the children's library on 5 July 1949 the youngsters took their own adventurous tour. Inspired by the wall frieze a boy scoured the shelves, looking for the latest Biggles adventure. The daring wartime exploits of the character created by Captain WE Johns were a must for any lad wanting to share the excitement of the skies, looping the loop and machine gunning Messerschmitts at will. These tales remained popular long after the war and even inspired a television series in the 1960s, starring John Leyton. The girls pored over stories of fairies and goblins or the adventures of the 'Famous Five on Treasure Island', one of a stream of children's stories from the pen of Enid Blyton. In later years her work would become unpopular with the powers that be. Trendy teachers and councils banned her books because they were not politically correct. Never mind that children loved them, grew up on them and used the text to inspire a love of books. Instead, the library and classroom bookshelves had to accommodate tomes about Wayne and Jason living together and rearing Tracey. Fortunately, educationalists saw sense, reintroducing Janet and John style readers, but for a generation the damage had been done. Not many young people today list reading as one of their hobbies. Half a century ago you had to prise a child's head out of a book, so enthralling were the stories and the rich images they conjured up.

Right: Fiddles, squeezeboxes, guitars and double basses provided the music for the annual country dance party in Stewart Park. Mrs Dorothy Davidge kept things moving along with a swing as she 'called the tune'. During the day over 2,000 children took part in the event, dancing to the music provided by a small folk dance band made up of teachers and senior pupils. The band was led by the schools' music organiser, Mr E Raymond, into a variety of numbers guaranteed to keep toes tapping and hands clapping. The local primary school dancers, the youngest being just six, learned the steps and turns in their PE classes. Schools' radio broadcasts, relayed through the tannoy in the main hall, helped teachers guide their pupils through traditional country dances that were once a regular Saturday night feature in every village hall. In the late 1970s schools replaced the teaching of formal dance steps with something called 'Movement, music and mime'. It involved a group of children standing in the middle of the hall pretending to be trees blown about in the wind, usually accompanied by another set acting as a rippling brook. Although country dancing made a modest comeback in the 1990s, we now have a generation that thinks it gains something out of life by hugging sycamores or listening to a CD by Enya.

Bottom: According to the Beach Boys, the 60s were 'Fun, fun, fun', or at least until daddy took the T-Bird away. The youngsters were enjoying themselves in Stewart Park on 24 June 1966, but their fun was not connected with hot rod cars or surfing in California. They participated in the traditional English ritual of country dancing, showing off their Cumberland reels and eightsomes. Here the children promenaded two by two, no doubt on their way under an arch formed by the first couple in the line. Then they Oxo-ed, threw in a right hand turn, followed by a left hand star and generally had a whale of a time. Now that they have all grown up to be parents, have they encouraged their offspring to follow in their footsteps? Let us hope that they did not surrender to their infants' demands and allow them to become whingeing brats playing computer games and annoying everyone around them sending text messages on their mobile phones. Country dancing in the park was hugely popular, as can be seen from the hundreds participating. Other than some music and a caller to shout out the moves, no equipment was needed. Just grab a partner and here we go, swing her to the left and then do-si-do. Turn your partner and tap those feet, move down one to the square dance beat!

Above: There is something about gently rippling water that is so soothing to the breast. That must be why we get relaxation and satisfaction from hanging over a railing, merely gazing at the water lapping so peacefully in front of us. The railings were not there initially, but so many children fell into the lake meant their introduction on safety grounds. The fishermen did not try too hard to catch anything, their rods an excuse to idle away a few hours away from the hurly burly of life outside Albert Park. The feathered friends on the boating lake regarded the little motor and rowing boats as just other species of water creatures, so often did they appear. Rowing boats had been a feature of the park as far back as 1876. Just in case they got too close, a rope strung across the water protected the ducks and geese, acting as a territorial boundary. The park was a gift to the public from Henry Bolckow. On 11 August 1868 Prince Arthur of Connaught, the seventh child of Queen Victoria, performed the ceremonial opening, naming the park in honour of his father, Prince Albert. He had died seven years earlier and the Queen was keen to respect his memory by seeing as many parks, streets and buildings named after him as was humanly possible.

Below: It was best bib and tucker at the Highfield Hotel on 28 January 1966. Later known as The Halfpenny, the hotel was originally a villa when it was built in 1874. The well appointed Highfield on Marton Road, in its own grounds that faced Easson Street, was a popular venue for important dinners. This occasion was the annual dinner of the Chartered Shipbrokers. Waiting to go into the dining room, JE Kynaston (secretary), FN Simpson (vice chairman), JSB Gentry (general manager of the Tees Conservancy Commission), Herbert Joyce (national chairman), Alderman T Farthing (mayor) and NRM Moir (chairman) chatted about the state of shipbuilding and what the future held. Perhaps they also discussed the major news events of the time that were breaking at that time. Mrs Indira Gandhi had just been elected Prime Minister of India. Fancy that, a woman in charge of a government. As the shipbrokers discussed those happenings they could not imagine such a thing happening in Britain in their lifetime. Yet a grocer's daughter from Grantham, a junior backbencher in the Commons would have emerged as the most powerful political figure in the country before the next decade ended.

Bird's eye view

The aerial shot is of one of Middlesbrough's best known and well loved landmarks, the Transporter Bridge, or 'Tranny' as it is affectionately known. So popular has it become and so far reaching its reputation, that a special visitors' centre has been established on Ferry Road. Here tourists and school parties learn about the history of the bridge and the surrounding area of St Hilda's. They will discover that the Transporter was built to ferry vehicles and pedestrians across the river, whilst being high enough to allow tall ships to pass underneath when not in use. Dominating the skyline, it is the only working bridge of its type in the country. With a central span of 570 feet and 220 feet high at its uppermost point, the total length of 850 feet was formally opened on 19 October 1911. Prince Arthur of Connaught, one of Queen Victoria's grandsons, presided at the ceremony that was also attended by the mayor, Sir Hugh Bell. Later in the day he planted a tree in Albert Park, next to one put there by his father, also Prince Arthur, 43 years earlier. The Transporter Bridge was built by Arroll's, a Glaswegian company, at a cost of £84,000. It was heavily used by workers on their way to the ironworks and dockyards, as well as day trippers off to Seaton Carew. Illuminated at night in the winter months, the bridge gleams as a beacon to the heritage of the industries that made Middlesbrough's name.

The railway line branches off to the right towards Saltburn and down to Whitby, away from the station on the left. The old town grew up on the far side of the tracks, around the former market square and town hall near the top right of the photograph. From here North Street, East Street, West Street and South Street led out in straight lines, faithful to the town plan drawn up in 1829. The interlinking street pattern, based on those planned grid lines, continued out as more and more housing was built to accommodate the workers drawn to the area by the burgeoning coal, and later iron, industries. It seems hard to imagine that there were just four farms in this vicinity at the start of the 19th century. Materials from Middlesbrough Priory were used to build the house at Middlesbrough Farm from where Edward and Joseph Pease accessed the coal staiths and helped lay out the town. When the Darlington to Stockton railway was extended those extra few miles to Middlesbrough, a task completed on 27 December 1830, the real story of the town was ready to begin. Railway workers, mining employees and sailors poured in, shipyards and iron industries were established and Middlesbrough was on its way to a dominant position in the industrial revolution.

This aerial view of Smith's Dock Company Limited is a reminder of the days in which it was a vibrant yard, busy with shipping along its front and in the dry docks. The work went hand in glove with the neighbouring iron and steel industries, matching their rise in importance to the economy of Teesside. But with the highs come corresponding lows as both industries went into decline. Smith's Dock Company was born on Tyneside in 1899 with the merger of three shipyards, Edwards Brothers, T and W Smith and HS Edwards and Sons, being established in Middlesbrough in 1908. The company had its work cut out building the dock as this part of South Bank

was a stretch of unfriendly mudflats. To build up the dock 160,000 cubic feet of slag was used in readiness for its opening for business on 8 February 1909. The first ships to use its facilities were berthed in dry docks, shipbuilding not being initiated until the following year. The 'Priestman', a dredger, had the privilege of being the first one to be built here. Smith's Dock countered the depression years of the 1920s by converting merchant ships into whalers, developing into a flourishing concern that gave jobs to the local workforce and helped smaller associated businesses to prosper in its wake. Now the only wake is the one held for the soul of a once great industry.

From this aerial view the shopping and commercial heart of the centre can be seen on Linthorpe Road and Albert Road, as Grange Road and Newport Road join them across. Middlesbrough grew from virtually nothing to a thriving, busy town in a few short decades. Its rise in importance led Prime Minister Gladstone to describe it as an 'infant Hercules', reflecting how the town had gone from strength to strength. A population of less than 8,000 in the 1850s had swollen to over 55,000 when the 1881 census was taken and the new town centre, seen below, supplanted the original St Hilda's area as the focus of attention. In the late 19th and early 20th centuries the town's boundaries were frequently being extended, absorbing neighbouring communities and boroughs. By the 1960s the population had risen to over 150,000 and changes in local government meant that the County Borough of Middlesbrough became part of the new Teesside County Borough. That was further amended in 1974, when Middlesbrough Borough Council was revived as part of the new county of Cleveland, and again in 1996 when it became a unitary council once more. Parts of the town centre have been pedestrianised since this photograph was taken, making shopping an easier and more pleasant experience than when car exhausts came alongside carrier bags.

Newport Road and Corporation Street run diagonally left to right across the picture where the Town Hall and Municipal Buildings can be seen to the right. The foundation stone was laid on 24 October 1883, but it was over five years later, in 1889, that the work was completed. Built to a design by George Hoskins of Darlington, the cost of £130,000 seems modest in today's figures, but in Victorian England it amounted to considerable investment. The Prince and Princess of Wales, the future King Edward VII and Queen Alexandra, presided at the opening ceremony. They had spent the previous night at Aske Hall, Richmond, before travelling on the royal train to be greeted by the official welcoming party at the railway station. From there they came in a carriage and four past cheering crowds along streets lined with bunting and waving flags. This aerial view of the Town Hall was taken across the roof of the Cleveland Centre that was under construction at the time. Various plans to revamp town centre shopping were considered during the 1960s, a public inquiry and exhibitions were held and ministerial approval sought before the final die was cast. Building work began in July 1969, but it took several years to complete the original development as work was carried out in three phases. By the end of 1973, 318,000 square feet of retail space had been filled.

Sporting life

'**H**oratio on the blower' could be the title of a CS Forrester book about his intrepid naval hero doing battle with the French. The chap in the picture, however, did his sailing through soccer defences, splitting them apart with a drop of the shoulder, a shimmy and an accurate pass. Horatio Stratton Carter, the 'Maestro' to his fans, was born in Sunderland on 21 December 1913. Known to everyone as 'Raich', he followed in his father's footsteps as a professional footballer. Even though he was a schoolboy international, Leicester City rejected him as being too small. Their loss was Sunderland's gain when his home town snapped him up in 1930. By the age of 24 he had won every domestic trophy and medal going, including being capped by his country when only 20. He only played in 13 full internationals, spending what should have been his peak years in wartime service. Raich joined Derby County in 1946, becoming the only man to gain FA Cupwinner's medals either side of the war. He went to Hull City as player manager in 1948, later managing Leeds United and Mansfield Town. In January 1963 Raich was appointed manager of Middlesbrough, but his sacking in February 1966 left him disillusioned with football and he was lost to the game. Since 9 October 1994 Raich Carter has been playing left half for a heavenly team that includes Stanley Matthews, Duncan Edwards and Bobby Moore.

Below: Football at its grassroots, or to be more correct at its mud base, is where it all begins for budding stars of the game. For most, that is where it remains. For every lad who makes it into the big time there are thousands of others who continue to play the national game in front of two men and a dog. Every weekend the parks and public pitches are full of young, and not so young, men loving every minute of chasing a ball around a field. Some, like Brian Glover in 'Kes', live out imaginary roles as superstars, deluding themselves that they could have made the grade if only they had been able to have that lucky break. What if a scout from the 'Boro had been watching the day I curled one into the top corner from the edge of the box? The players giving their all at Clairville in February 1960 were young hopefuls trying to impress the selectors from the English Schools FA. A series of trials was held, up and down the country, to try to find the best talent to represent the national team at schoolboy level. North Midlands' goalie, J Leadbitter, threw himself bravely at the feet of the North's onrushing forward, D Allnut. In later years he would come to think that even Gordon Banks could not have done better that day, so why did Alf Ramsey pick him in 1966?

Below: To me, to you, on me 'ead, son! In the days before isotonic drinks, state of the art training centres and schools of excellence, professional soccer players practised their skills quite simply in humble surroundings. Not for them a few days in a Spanish training camp as they prepared for a big match, the sands at Redcar would have to do. On a bleak January day in 1966 the first team squad limbered up in readiness for the FA Cup tie at White Hart Lane the following Saturday. That was the day of the week when football fans used to go to a match, listen to the results on radio's 'Sports Report' and read a description of the game in the evening paper. Since the coming of satellite television, nothing is ever finalised on a Saturday at 4.40 pm. Games kick off in the morning, Sunday afternoon, Monday evening or at any other time that the TV moguls decide. This trio of Middlesbrough players belonged to a time in football now known as BM, before Murdoch. Dickie Rooks, Gordon Jones and Arthur Horsfield were looking forward to pitting their skills against the mighty Tottenham. Rooks was the centre half bought from Sunderland for £17,000, later moving to Bristol City for the same amount. Jones had a distinguished career with 'Boro, becoming the team captain and playing over 500 games for the club. Centre forward Horsfield flickered in and out of the side for six seasons, though he did play over 100 times. There was no happy ending to the time at Redcar as Spurs won the tie 4-0, one of many poor results that year that sent Middlesbrough tumbling into Division Three.

There was great excitement in the country in 1966 as soccer's World Cup competition came to England for the only time in its history. Group games were scattered across the country, giving soccer outposts the chance to witness at first hand some of the game's finest players. Middlesbrough fans were delighted when Ayresome Park was selected as the venue for some of the preliminary games. North Korea, Russia, Chile and Italy were the sides competing for the two qualifying places into the quarter finals. By the time the last matches were to be played, Russia had claimed one spot and the other would be decided by the result of the North Korea v Italy game. The World Cup has seen some shock defeats, usually involving Scotland, but the one on 19 July 1966 ranks amongst the biggest. The terraces were far from full, only 18,727 attending the game, but they witnessed a result that sent the Italians home to a welcome party at the airport more in keeping with one reserved for serial killers. The Koreans, none of whom stood much taller than a corner flag, won 1-0, Pak Doo Ik scoring late in the first half. North Korea progressed to the next round, where another major shock was on the cards for a while. A 3-0 lead over Portugal was established, but the Koreans ran out of steam as the mighty Eusebio took the game by the scruff of the neck to engineer a 5-3 victory. The Koreans were out, but not forgotten.

On the move

Was this the inspiration for 'Roll out the barrel' or even Lonnie Donegan's 1956 hit about a tollgate on the 'Rock Island Line'? The lorry, belonging to the haulage firm of Fred Robinson of Stamp Street in Stockton, was getting up a head of steam as it prepared to leave the toll bar at Cargo Fleet, South Bank Road. Situated close to where football fans now stream into the Riverside Stadium, those supporters now pay a lot more to pass through the turnstiles than it cost to negotiate the right of way owned by Lord Furness. Tolls were in frequent use, raising income for the landowner to spend on the upkeep of the section of a road that lay inside his estates. Many roads were in private ownership, even in the 20th century. The toll bars were a nuisance to the free flow of traffic, causing frequent interruptions on a single journey. The payments to the keeper increased the overheads for commercial vehicles and were thoroughly unpopular with everyone other than those raking in the profits. The feeling was common throughout Britain wherever road tolls were levied, spilling over into violent objection as witnessed in the Rebecca Riots in the 19th century in southwest Wales. It was only in 1916 that private tollgates were abolished when councils became irritated that vital equipment for the war effort was being delayed.

Below: The Tees was once alive with ferry boats, working barges and paddle steamers plying their trade the length and breadth of its waters. At times there seemed to be a flotilla of craft bobbing up and down, backwards and forwards, as they went weaving their way on both commercial and pleasure journeys. From afar they looked like so many dark corks rising and falling in the water. At times they were so numerous it was hard to even see a clear stretch of river. The 'Camperdown', built in 1868, was one of the many paddle steamers that worked the river. Large steamers like the 'Hugh Bell' and the 'Erimus' could cater for 800-900 passengers at a time. The paddle steamer was a highly efficient form of transport, competitive even with modern propellers. However, the wheel was liable to damage in stormy weather and steering was not easy in choppy conditions, demanding extra skills from the helmsman. When paddle steamers are mentioned today we immediately think of the showboats and gambling decks of those that operated on the Mississippi. But, the Tees was also once home to these relics of the past. We may not have had dancing girls and Maverick dealing hands of poker at the card tables, but we had our own version of that craft immortalised on a bottle of Southern Comfort.

Bottom right: In 1950 bobbies on bicycles were common sights on our streets as they patrolled the town and suburbs keeping the peace. Each police officer knew his patch well, including a lot about the lives of the people who lived there. Naughty children avoided formal visits to the police station thanks to a common sense approach where a clip on the back of the head or a quiet word in dad's ear avoided a visit to the juvenile court. A swift dispensing of justice these days would see the copper in court and the youth screaming, 'I'll sue!'

The row of bikes, propped up in the shed at the municipal buildings, reminds us of Mr Plod and Noddy, but that cannot be the latter's little car. Was the chief constable visiting or was the owner a forerunner of Chief Inspector Morse or Sergeant Bergerac, those popular television policemen who loved flashy cars? Heaven help the humble PC 49 whose pedal scratched the gleaming coachwork as he pedalled off on his beat or he would be on point duty for the rest of his shift. The police headquarters moved to shiny new premises on the other side of Victoria Gardens in 1962, also moving into a generation of Z cars rather than Dixon of Dock Green.

Top right: Trams can still be seen on English roads as they make their comeback in Croydon, Manchester, Sheffield, Newcastle and several other towns. Middlesbrough is unlikely to see their return, so generations of locals can only imagine what it was like to travel on the clanking public transport that bowed out in the 1930s. In their time they were an efficient mode of transport, but the coming of petrol engined buses, not tied to railtracks, tolled their death knell. This car, with advertising for Binns department store on its front, is seen at the Exchange Place terminus, making the run on the Linthorpe to Transporter route for the last time on 9 June 1934. The official opening of the electric tram

service took place on 16 July 1898 amid much excitement for the dawn of a new age. Townspeople had been accustomed to horse drawn carriages and even a few steam powered vehicles, but the magic of electricity humming through the wires provided a clean and reliable service that seemed set to revolutionise public transport. How ironic it would be that the cleanliness of the fuel that powered the tram was to give way to the pollution laden engines of the motor bus in just a few decades. Optimism still ran high when the Teesside Bridge Engineering Company built new tram sheds for the Corporation, opened by Councillor Edwin Turner in July 1922, not knowing that another 12 years were all that were left.

The Tees has witnessed many strange vessels travelling through its waters from paddle steamers to fully rigged sailing ships, from tug boats to battle cruisers. On 26 August 1966 it saw one of the oddest craft to leave Teesside, the Trans-Ocean Number Two oil drilling rig. In the 1960s and 1970s Britain's economy was helped by the exploitation of huge fields of oil and natural gas found in the North Sea. Large platforms were sailed out to the sites of these rich sources of energy, deep shafts were sunk and pipelines to the mainland laid. The workers on board the rigs earned high wages and many towns on the east coast of England and Scotland benefited from the boom. The men tapping into these new reserves earned their fat pay packets because of the dangers of working in such a volatile environment. In April 1977 lifeboats rescued 100 workers from the platform of the Bravo rig in the Ekofisk Field when it blew out of control. Worse was to follow, as in March 1980 half of the 200 men on board the Alexander Kielland, being used as a floating hotel for rig workers, capsized in rough seas. Other tragedies, including the Piper Alpha fire in July 1988 that killed 167, served to remind the world that the sea does not surrender her treasures cheaply.

The large 'NO' painted on the road says everything about messages given out to the poor motorist. You cannot turn right here, left there, enter this road or go along that bus lane. There are bumps in the carriageway to slow you down and hatching in the middle of the road to make sure you cannot overtake even the most tortoise-like vehicle. If only there was a road marking somewhere that said 'YES', you can come along here, you are welcome to take this turning or please do park somewhere to your own convenience. To quote both John Wayne and Buddy Holly, 'That'll be the day'. Those drivers who are also smokers must feel as if they are being hit by a double whammy, or is it paranoia setting in? Near the railway crossing, the lorry coming down Sussex Street towards Linthorpe Road will have to do as it is told and turn according to the arrowed instruction. Approaching Cohen's scrapyard, it has just passed the Crown Hotel, in the centre of the photograph, a landmark on the corner of Bridge Street for nearly 150 years. It opened for business in 1839, but was demolished in 1986. Further on the gable end of the RC Cathedral is just visible, but it, too, is no more, being destroyed by fire in 2000.

Shopping spree

Below left: The pace of life was so gentle on Corporation Street in 1923. People could promenade along the road with only the occasional car to disturb their equilibrium. It was still a period when horse drawn vehicles were as common as petrol driven ones. People bobbed about on bicycles as the old and new orders lived happily side by side. Public transport underwent an earlier change when electricity was harnessed instead of the noble steed to carry passengers to their destinations. Travel on the earliest trams could be a damp and draughty affair as the upper decks were open to the elements. For many years, even after the tops were enclosed, drivers sat in open cabs at the front, steeling themselves against icy rain and piercing winds. Middlesbrough had a mixture of single and double decker trams, the former being used on routes that had low bridges, such as Albert Bridge on the Linthorpe route. Nostalgia abounds for the days of the tram, even though there are not many of us left who ever travelled on one. By the time Judy Garland sang her 'Trolley song' in the 1944 film 'Meet me in St Louis' she had missed the last tram in Middlesbrough by 10 years. They and their tracks had been taken to the scrapyard and gone somewhere 'Over the rainbow'.

Bottom: By 1960 car ownership had become far more common as the country's prosperity grew. Ordinary folk were able to afford what had been the province of the middle classes, but there would be another price to pay. This junction of Albert Road and Corporation Road was just a foretaste of what was to come as the volume of traffic grew. The motorists who had parked their cars had to enjoy the privilege while they could, because parking meters and no waiting signs would be making their presence felt before the end of the decade. The British car industry was well represented in this picture, with hardly a whiff of the foreign invasion that would come. Riley, Morris, Austin and Hillman became the names of yesterday when Mazda, Nissan, Toyota and Honda came to call. In 1960 we had home grown pleasures to enjoy that complemented the delight of motoring along in a British built car. At the cinema, London's very own Elizabeth Taylor had cracked Hollywood and would win an Oscar for her performance in 'Butterfield Eight'. There was a new musical around, the first proper British one since the days of Ivor Novello, that had a whole clutch of tuneful songs. Lionel Bart's 'Oliver', with its jaunty cast of pickpockets, would later transfer from the stage to film with huge success in 1968.

Above: Saturday was more than just the day you went into town to do your shopping, it was a chance to meet friends, catch up on the gossip and blow away the work day blues. The pavements were as crowded with window shoppers as they were with people really intent on making a purchase. Pretty girls in floral prints, young men in suits and open necked shirts enjoyed the sunshine and each other's company. Lovers strolled hand in hand, gazing into the jeweller's display cases, wondering if a visit inside would be on the cards very soon. Little knots of people chinwagged on the street corner and there was not a piece of litter to be seen. You certainly never ate in the street, that was far too common for the likes of us, we popped into a tearoom for a cuppa and a scone. There we could talk happily about the world's events, why 'Boro had lost at home again or how shocking it was that the next door neighbour's daughter had been out until after midnight. As we looked out to the pavement and beyond there was just a sea of activity, so many people and so much traffic. It was accepted as part of our lifestyle, for what did it matter that it took an age to get through the traffic jam or past the hordes under the shop awnings? This was Saturday and there was no work today, nor any tomorrow. Monday would come soon enough, so we put it to the back of our minds and concentrated on enjoying the weekend.

In the early 1960s the large buildings belonging to British Home Stores and Binns stood proudly on the corner of Corporation Road and Linthorpe Road. Stand in the same spot now, as the photographer did then, and point your camera towards Newport Street. When the snap is developed you will find that some things hardly ever change, despite all the alterations to shopping habits. Although the new BHS logo now adorns the shop on the left, it is still essentially the same business, as is the store opposite. The prices on the goods on display have changed significantly, and not just because of inflation. In the 60s everything was in pounds, shillings and pence and most things had quaint price tags, for they all seemed to end in 11d. We knew that 9s 11d was only a penny less than ten bob, but it sounded so much cheaper! The restrictions on traffic along here had already started, as can be seen from the 'No waiting' signs, in a first attempt to clear the streets of parked cars that used to clog the flow. Just to re-emphasise the point, the council put up two signs within yards of each other, making sure that there was no excuse for failing to spot that this was no place to leave your car. Of course, the motorist had to be accommodated somewhere, hence the arrival of that monstrosity, the multi storey car park.

In the autumn of 1966 drinkers were still getting used to the keg beers that were being introduced into our pubs. Younger's Tartan, being advertised on the hoarding on Garnet Street, vied with Watney's Red Barrel for popularity, but these brews were not to everybody's taste as oldtimers turned up their noses at the pressurised pint being put before them. More youthful suppers did not know what they were missing, compared with the hand drawn beer that used to flow through the pumps. Landlords quite liked the new ales as they were easier to look after, seldom leading a customer to bring a glass back to the bar with a complaint that he had been given a cloudy draught. Traditionalists joined CAMRA, the campaign for real ale, in an effort to stem the tide of what they regarded as a tasteless liquid, totally lacking both body and character. It is still active today, trying to promote variety by supporting small breweries in the face of competition from the giant corporations. Across from the advert, Upton's store on Linthorpe Road was doing good business, but it suffered in later years when the large shopping centres in the town centre were opened. Retail focus shifted back along the road, leaving this outlet of the business that Edward Upton founded in 1869 as a small grocery in South Bank having to work hard to survive.

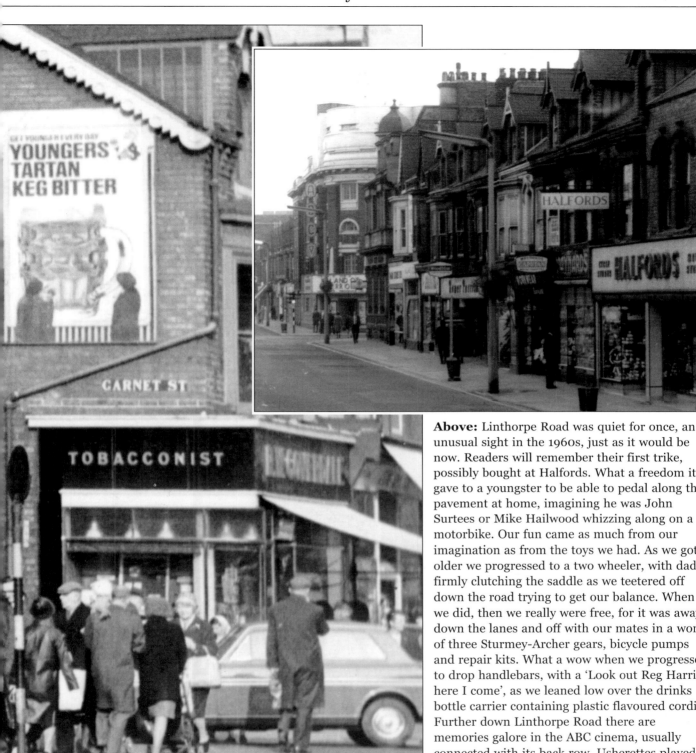

Above: Linthorpe Road was quiet for once, an unusual sight in the 1960s, just as it would be now. Readers will remember their first trike, possibly bought at Halfords. What a freedom it gave to a youngster to be able to pedal along the pavement at home, imagining he was John Surtees or Mike Hailwood whizzing along on a motorbike. Our fun came as much from our imagination as from the toys we had. As we got older we progressed to a two wheeler, with dad firmly clutching the saddle as we teetered off down the road trying to get our balance. When we did, then we really were free, for it was away down the lanes and off with our mates in a world of three Sturmey-Archer gears, bicycle pumps and repair kits. What a wow when we progressed to drop handlebars, with a 'Look out Reg Harris, here I come', as we leaned low over the drinks bottle carrier containing plastic flavoured cordial. Further down Linthorpe Road there are memories galore in the ABC cinema, usually connected with its back row. Usherettes played their torches over the seats from time to time, just to make sure there was no real hanky panky going on, then transformed into waitresses carrying tubs of ice cream and a drink on a stick in those heavy trays slung from over their shoulders. If you were not treated to a choc ice, the usherettes would not need their torches, because your date had blown his chance!

The men anxiously checking the traffic as they cross Linthorpe Road need not do so any more, as this whole area is now pedestrianised. Shopping patterns have changed greatly in the years since this 1969 view was snapped as malls and arcades, such as the Hill Street Centre behind this row, have been added to the lines of individual shops we used to know. Whilst the premises have been retained, many of the names over the doors have changed. But not everything associated with the past has disappeared, for Marks and Spencer still trades from here, continuing to supply quality goods.

The company has struggled, of late, weighed down by an image that it could not keep up with modern trends, especially in clothing. But, as the swinging 60s came to an end, it was very popular with those who wanted something other than the latest Carnaby Street fads. Mini skirts, hot pants and flowery patterns made their impact in boutiques then and in the early 1970s, but there was still a large market for practical and sensible clothing. Yet there was a swing towards more casual wear as men did not bother to come into town sporting ties, women dressed in trousers and children put on something other than their school uniforms.

At work

The warning to speeding drivers seems obvious, there being little room to fit under the railway bridge. The Sussex Street subway in 1928 was one of the links between the old town, where the first houses were built, and the town that developed south of the railway. The Darlington to Stockton line was extended as far as Redcar in 1846. The first Middlesbrough station was then built, being replaced by a larger affair in 1877. The £100,000 cost provided the town with a building that was striking, particularly for its stylish arched glass and iron roof. That was badly damaged in the war and the basic, functional replacement roof makes the present station appear is if it has been built in a mixture of architectural styles. The appeal of the station to the artistic eye, or the neat patterns worked upon Sussex Street bridge, did not interest the cyclist as he made his way to work. He was happy to be in employment, as so many others felt the pinch of the depression years that led to the general strike in 1926 when miners had their pay cut. In America, a year after this photograph was taken, the Wall Street stock market crashed, throwing many into financial ruin. Unemployment, low wages, strikes and financial crisis were not what the government promised us after the first world war. This was supposed to be a 'land fit for heroes'.

If you suffer from vertigo turn over this page very quickly and ignore the temptation to look down! Just a glance at the two workmen perched at the top of this structure is enough to give you the willies. If ever the payment of danger money was justified, this is it. Perched high above the river in 1932 this intrepid pair ignored the buffeting wind sweeping up the Tees. They were engaged in the construction of the Newport Bridge, the first vertical lift bridge in the country. Local firm Dorman Long provided the expertise in building it at a cost of £512,000. The Duke and Duchess of York officiated at the ceremonial opening on 28 February 1934 of the world's heaviest bridge of its type. The lifting span and counter balance weigh a massive 5,400 tons, supported by towers that rise 200 feet into the sky. Newport Bridge had been a pipe dream for ten years after the first world war, until plans were at long last pushed through by Middlesbrough Council to provide an alternative to the Transporter Bridge. Unfortunately, it was decided, as a cost cutting exercise, to fix the bridge at road level and it made its last 99 foot raise on 18 November 1990.

Above: Hard, manual graft in any ironworks was a hot, sweaty affair, putting a strain on sinews and muscles. The temperatures could rise to degrees that saw men lose pounds in perspiration during a single shift. These men were employees of the nationally famous Dorman Long Company, seen here in January 1930 working with their ladles, emptying slag into rail hoppers for transporting to the slagheaps. There they became part of the unattractive landscape that blighted the view before landscaping was ever thought of. The company's history goes back into Victorian times, to 1875 when Arthur Dorman and Albert de Lande Long took out a lease on the West Marsh Iron Works. Although capable of producing 240 tons of wrought iron bars on a weekly basis, the partners knew they had to expand production in order to prosper. Within four years they had taken over the Britannia Works, rolled their first steel joists and established the business on the sure footing that made it one of the best known in Britain. Dorman Long became a limited company in 1889, going from strength to strength. One of its most notable ventures came in the late 1920s when it was commissioned to build the Sydney Harbour Bridge that opened in 1932. With a main arch span of 1,650 feet, it is one of the longest steel-arch, single span bridges in the world. When the industry was nationalised in 1967, Dorman Long came under the umbrella of British Steel.

Below: When we see buildings being demolished today it is usually a job that requires explosives or a crane swinging a huge ball. Piles of rubble, clouds of dust and everything comes hurtling to the ground in an undignified heap. This pair of workers adopted a more careful approach to the task in hand in 1935. Perched on the roof, they took time and trouble dismantling a terrace of white cottages on St Barnabas Road, Linthorpe, the former cemetery road. How many memories did they unpick as they removed the roofing nails and slates? Despite their efforts in treating the homes with dignity, the result was still the same. By the time they left the site, little remained of this small part of semi rural old England. Attitudes in the 21st century would have seen the cottages preserved, renovated and sold on by developers as bijou residences. Not so in the 1930s, for old properties stood in the way of progress. Linthorpe kept its own sense of identity until the early years of the 20th century. Wealthy professional classes and merchants who had made their pile settled in the area, making it an exclusive zone for some. Eventually, further building blurred the boundary edges and Linthorpe was swallowed up by the town, making it just another suburb.

Those much missed comedians Morecambe and Wise, so hugely popular for a quarter of a century until Eric Morecambe's death in 1984, used to tell a gag about two old men in deckchairs. When Eric and Ernie were learning their trade they should have come to Victoria Square on 30 September 1948. They would have been able to come up with a routine about seven old men on a park bench. The oldtimers sat glumly watching another piece of Middlesbrough history being dismantled. For years they had come to sit here and listen to a variety of music to soothe even the most fevered brow. Bands played 'Liberty Bell' and other stirring Sousa marches, interspersed with songs from the shows and Gilbert and Sullivan evergreens. The band of the Coldstream Guards played the first notes that were heard coming from the bandstand in July 1901. They played some jaunty ditties that reflected the mood of the country as it moved from the Victorian era into an Edwardian age of greater frivolity. As the workmen removed the bandstand, bit by bit, the watchers put the world to rights in their conversation. As they gazed across at the Hugh Bell School complex, they remarked on the success of Fanny Blankers-Koen in winning four gold medals at the London Olympics in August. Their conclusion was that she should have been at home, doing the housework and looking after the children.

Above: The equipment might look like something Heath Robinson dreamt up, but this was state of the art hospital operating theatre equipment in March 1936. The nurse was proudly tending the site where new lives would enter the world, for this was in the main wing of the maternity hospital on Park Road North. A major remodelling exercise had just been completed, providing extensions that offered additional wards and staff accommodation. The hospital opened in July 1920, at a time when childbirth usually took place at home. The midwife, lashings of hot water, clean towels and a prayer were all that were needed to introduce another mouth to feed into the family. Infant mortality was not as high as in the previous century, when bad housing conditions, a poor diet and disease contributed to so many deaths. Even so, having a baby was still a bigger risk for both mother and child than it is in today's world with its free welfare, painkillers and modern drugs. In 1936, mum gritted her teeth and got on with it. Dad paced the floor outside, keeping out of the way of the nursing staff who regarded his presence on the corridor as a proper nuisance. Any idea of being included in the birthing process going on in the operating theatre would have given matron apoplexy.

Above: A woman's work is never done. It never will be, if men have their way. Wives and girlfriends are pressed into service to provide teas at cricket matches, put on refreshments for card schools and take care of all the catering arrangements at church fítes. It is only of late that they have had the courage to say, 'Get your own'. The days of burning bras and women's lib had not fully dawned in July 1966, so it was on with the rubber gloves and pass the tea towel, pet. There was washing up to be done for 900, but they dare not think about the size of the task or the first seeds of rebellion might just have been sown. The reason for their hard work was to show support for the nine day event that began on 9 July. Planning for the activities was co-ordinated at the Central Chambers, Albert Road, under the chairmanship of S Jenkins Evans and the general secretary, Emrys Roberts. Careful of examination of their names gives a clue as to the nature of the event. It was the occasion of the Teesside International Industrial Eisteddfod, when leeks, Druids and red dragons held sway in Middlesbrough in a celebration of Gallic culture. 'Men of Harlech' was sung with gusto, though with less fervour by these women. Well, they had to clean up after them, and the men of Cardiff, Swansea, Wrexham and Barmouth to boot.

The cranes on Smith's Dock could be part of a formation dancing team or part of a giant modern sculpture, so artistic is the pose in this photograph. Set against the background of blue skies and wispy white clouds, the metallic giants have a ghostly feel about them. There was nothing romantic about the day when that feel became reality, for on 28 February 1987 the dock closed its gates for the final time. The writing had been on the wall for some years, especially after the 1980 closure of Middlesbrough Dock. In the war Middlesbrough dockers fiercely defended their record in turning round cargo ships quicker than any of their counterparts could manage. The shipyards were kept at full stretch meeting the demands of the war effort, producing Mulberry harbours and corvettes for the Royal Navy. But, once the war ended, the great years of activity on the waterfront went into decline. By the 1960s the industry was in real trouble, though an order to build four container ships for Manchester Liners helped stay the executioner's axe. There was a comeback in the 1970s as orders for Finnish refrigerated vessels and eight reefers for Island Fruit Reefers Limited kept things going. No such luck helped Smith's Dock in the 1980s and the grim reaper entered centre stage.

A racing cert

How many Middlesbrough residents enjoy a flutter on the horses? Rather a lot, even if it is only once a year on the Grand National.

For decades the name Reg Boyle has been a familiar one to Middlesbrough's race lovers.

Reg Boyle became hooked on betting at an early age when he bet threepence each way on Golden Fox which won at odds of 100-7. Reg's first bet on a racecourse was at Thirsk during World War II; his first race winner there was Kings Jubilee at 8-1.

Christened Owen Boyle junior (and only later acquiring his nickname) Reg was the second youngest of five children born to Owen Boyle, an ex-professional footballer who had played for Bradford Park Avenue, and his wife Margaret.

Reg grew up at 34 Lower Napier Street, South Bank, Middlesbrough on the same street as Wilf Mannion. 'I always got a football for Christmas, often borrowed by Wilf and his pals to play on the 'Puddling' Reg recalled.

In 1940 after attending St Peters School, South Bank and St Mary's College Reg began work as a messenger boy at Cargo Fleet Steel Works and then became an apprentice pattern-maker. Reg started to take bets for a bookmaker on a commission basis and at the age of 17 he started up on his own - only to be soon cleaned out on the fixed odds football coupons and so returned to acting as an agent.

During World War II Reg was unable to join up as he was in a 'specified trade' but was called up later between 1946-48 when he represented the Army in two football matches in East Africa. After Army service, and a week at Butlins, Filey, Reg recklessly 'invested' the remainder of his Demob money, £110, on two bets and lost the lot to Alf Findlay. He decided then that it was much safer taking bets than making them!

Above left: *Founder Reg Boyle.*
Below: *Reg Boyle at Epsom Derby in the mid 1950s.*

Reg began taking bets in 1949 whilst still working at his trade of pattern-maker; in 1952 he opened a book on the racecourse with Tommy Dawson (an ex Charlton Athletic footballer who had been on the FA Cup winning team in 1947). In September 1952 Reg worked under his own name at the Doncaster St Leger meeting with a set of second hand equipment bought for £6 from bookmaker Tom Parkes. From the cheap rings Reg progressed through to the second rings: and in the winter he returned to his trade.

Unfortunately in September 1953 Reg was once more cleaned out on the fixed odds football coupons; he had to borrow £5 from his sister Madge for his travel, £1.50 single and lodging of £3 per week in advance to enable him to take up his trade in Birmingham where he worked until early 1954.

Still bitten by the betting bug Reg's big break came in 1956 when following a tip of from his friend Detective Constable Mick Finn he rented 22 Queen Street South Bank for £6 per week. The premises belonged to Ron Hislop who had recently ceased bookmaking. To help pay the rent Reg sold his Austin Somerset car.

On his first day Reg had only two customers: Alice Ford and Mrs Outhwaite who between them bet the princely sum of one pound and twelve shillings.

In 1957 Reg married local girl Irene Escritt. The couple would go on to have four children: daughters Susan, Angela and Lynne all of whom joined the family business from school whilst son Simon joined after attending university. The eldest daughter Susan became manageress at 19 years old.

The business became a company in May 1960. Until the Betting Act came into force in 1961 off-course betting was illegal, but the police allowed it to go on in certain areas provided it was conducted in an orderly manner (and it kept illegal gambling off the streets). One Saturday afternoon however when Reg and a clerk had a packed shop, the local police sergeant Ted Cockerill wandered in wearing full uniform. The place emptied in seconds; but all Ted wanted to do was place a half crown bet!

Above: *Reg Boyle collecting the Carlisle Bell in 1971.*
Below: *Reneé presenting Champagne to winners of The Reg Boyle Trophy, Redcar.*

In 1961 Reg Boyle was able to obtain licences for five shops in South Bank, Dormantstown and Saltburn. Reg Boyle Ltd would eventually run 26 shops in an area ranging from Ferryhill County Durham to Loftus in East Cleveland.

Reg's interest in horse racing extended from betting to sponsoring races at Teesside Park, Redcar and Sedgefield and to owning a number of successful horses. His first horse Kilindini won as a two year old at Ayr on her second outing in 1962. Reg bought her for 220 guineas and she went on to win four more races with prize money totalling more than £2,000 and was later sold for 1,800 guineas.

In 1971, in partnership with a friend Derek Hawkey, Reg won the Carlisle Bell the oldest race in Great Britain with El Credo. And Lester Piggott rode one of Reg's horses, Sir Blast, to the winners' enclosure in 1967 at Beverley.

Reg, as Owen Boyle jnr, became chairman of the now defunct Teesside and District Bookmakers Association and would later become a director of the Northern BPA. From 1965-1970 he would also be patron of South Bank Football Club and a

Prior to the Betting and Gaming Act of 1960 betting had been possible by telephone from street corners and with 'back alley' runners for bookmakers. Social and workingmen's clubs often had ticker tapes for the betting and results.

All this ceased on May 1st 1961 when the Betting Act came into force. In the Middlesbrough area more than 25 bookmakers received permits to operate, albeit from rather dismal premises due to the strict restrictions of the Act which didn't want to encourage surroundings which were too comfortable.

Shortly after the Betting Act came into force Reg and John Mallon were prosecuted for allowing a person under the age of 18 on licensed premises. The young man had been asked if he was 18 and had replied that he was and had just placed a bet when the police walked in. At court the accused were found not guilty. The case was the first of its kind and remains on record as the Crown versus 'Boyle and Mallon'.

Above and left: Reg and Reneé presenting winners of the Reg Boyle Trophy at Sedgefield. Below: Reg and Reneé with their extended family, including nine grandchildren, at the splendid Rushpool Hall, Saltburn, owned by a friend Jim Brennann, on the occasion of their Ruby Wedding Anniversary. This was a surprise party organised by their children and followed a Celebration Mass by Fr Ricardo Morgan at St Andrews, Teesville, 1997.

director of the South Bank Sporting Club, booking such famous acts as Tony Christie and the Penmen in 1969 for £125 per week, and for £120 per week Engelbert Humperdink, before he broke into the charts with 'Please Release Me'.

Reg was always a keen sportsman often playing local amateur football; at the age of 52 he took up running, winning races in his age group ranging from 10 miles to a marathon. Reg would raise many thousands of pounds for local and national charities through sponsorship and in 1986 was a nominee for Cleveland Sportsman of the Year.

The company had grown steadily since 1956 when annual turnover was just £18,672. Reg maintains that he was lucky to survive the early days of his business, due to lack of security. There was no hi-tech video and camera surveillance in those days and he would put the company's success down to faithful staff such as Phonsie, Hughie and John Mallon and the 15 agents with clock bags in the local docks, steelworks and ICI - and not least the constant support from his wife and company secretary Reneé.

In recent times the company has reorganised reducing the number of shops to 22 whilst undertaking an extensive refurbishment programme to create first class standards with air conditioning, large TV screens and many other creature comforts. The works were carried out by building contractor John Dunbar one of Reg's and Reneé's sons-in-law. New technology with the EPOS (Electronic Point of Sale) System and also a tax free internet site in conjunction with Beta-Bet.com would also be introduced.

Reg retired in 2001, after 49 years of racecourse bookmaking, however, he still remains active in the office.

Today all but three of the two dozen original independent bookmakers in Middlesbrough have been swallowed up by the big four.

But with ten grandchildren Reg Boyle can not only look back with pride but confidently take a bet that his family firm will still be in the bookmaking business for many more years to come.

Above left: *Reg and Reneé's daughter, Susan, presenting the Reg Boyle Trophy at Sedgefield.* ***Above:*** *Reneé and Reg presenting Champagne to the Head Lad of the winner of The Reg Boyle Sponsored Race, Redcar 1994.* ***Below:*** *Reg Boyle's Bookmakers, Acklam Road, Middlesbrough.*

It all started with a horse called Dina

AV Dawson Ltd is a Middlesbrough business with a world-wide reputation for offering import/export facilities by road, rail and sea. Serving customers on every continent and handling cargoes as diverse as mineral water to steel beams the company has the expertise and experience to satisfy the most demanding clients. Today, operating from sites at Dawsons Wharf, Ayrton Railhead and Store and North Sea Supply Base in Middlesbrough the company is the largest independent dry cargo wharf operator on the River Tees but how did this extraordinary business start?

Arthur Vernon Dawson, or 'Vernie' as he was universally known, started the company in 1938 with the help and support of Eleanor Dawson when they were both just 18 years old, they married a year later.

Vernie started out with the princely sum of £50, which he had raised by selling his much prized second hand car. With the money he bought a horse from Mr Dent, a farmer

from Hemlington. He bought shoes for the horse, whose name was Dina, and a cart for her to pull and a load of coal to sell - and he still had change out of his £50. Selling coal was a full-time occupation in the winter but during the summer months Dina used to carry light loads of haulage, furniture, timber and road construction materials. Despite it being war-time business soon grew and Vernie bought a lorry and Dina went into a well-earned retirement. With his new mode of transport, it was possible to

*Right: A newly delivered 9.6 litre AEC Majestic 6 wheel lorry. All the sign writing was in gold leaf and the Dawson Shield is still in use today. **Below:** Vernie's brother Jim Dawson pictured with Dina.*

haul coal direct from the coalfields of Durham and Northumberland. Coal was a rationed commodity and it was difficult for him to secure enough coal to meet the demand. The price of a cwt of coal back then, incidentally, was just 1/3d (6p).

Eleanor, as well as attending to everything at home, also undertook the book-keeping for the business and also drove the company lorries from time to time. This was necessary as many of the menfolk were away serving in His Majesty's Forces.

The coal business was however later sold to enable the fledgling firm to concentrate on road haulage, buying ex-army vehicles at first and new ones later. In 1956 Maurice Dawson, Vernie and Eleanor's son joined the growing company.

Not that being in the haulage business was easy. Vernie and Eleanor would never forget

Top: Posing for a family photograph in a borrowed MG sports car, Vernie, Eleanor, Maurice with Brenda the Alsation and the daughter of the car's owner. This picture was taken in Emmerson Street yard in 1947. Above: A new 150hp Atkinson 6 wheel lorry carrying a load of spun cast iron pipes on behalf of Cochranes iron foundry, circa 1952.

the way they spent their silver wedding anniversary. It was in court in London. The Northeast Licensing Authority had refused to grant them permission for additional tonnage and the couple challenged the decision. They won and celebrated the judgement and their wedding anniversary with a night out in London.

The business had been run from Emerson Street, now it was necessary to move to larger premises at Newport Road - later to be the home of Charlie Brown car parts. Soon this site too would be outgrown and the firm moved to Lloyd Street but with 45 vehicles on the road that site too became too small.

It was in 1973 that the Dawsons made one of the most significant moves in the firm's history when they arrived at their present base, then known as Middlesbrough Wharf, but later renamed Dawsons Wharf. The wharf is reported to be the oldest wharf on the river dating back to 1820 when it had been called Port Darlington and served the vast growing steel and ironworks which were being built nearby. The Dawsons acquired six acres of land to which they would soon add five more.

It was shortly after this period that Vernie was taken ill and stepped down as managing director and became

Nicholas hydraulic trailer was acquired from France - the combination cost £150,000.

Nor was that the only major investment. New roads were built on the 11 acre site and 30 small industrial units built. Alas such optimism was ill founded. Over the following three years British steel would shed 22,000 jobs and the area became a ghost town. Dawsons lost 6,000 tonnes per week of road haulage. It was time for diversification. Due to the loss of work for the haulage fleet the number of vehicles was reduced to just 12.

In 1985 the Ayrton Rolling Mill closed with the loss of 200 jobs. Dawsons purchased the site and used it to store potash - there were upwards of 20,000 tonnes of this with more on the way. That capacity was of interest to ICI which was looking for a place to store big bags of fertiliser. Dawsons had developed a means of lifting these with overhead cranes which could cope with 6 bags at a time. This was twice as efficient as the standard industry method and ICI was pleased to give Dawsons the contract to handle its goods.

Another major milestone passed in 1985 when after years of trying the company acquired a licence to operate the wharf which had been closed for many years. The licence was limited to loading bulk only, but it was enough to get Dawsons established in the business of handling ships.

1988, the 50th anniversary of the founding of the company, coincided with the official opening of the Ayrton Store and Rail Terminal; Michael Portillo opened it by driving into the site on the company's locomotive,

chairman. He never played an active role again at Middlesbrough but went on to build up a substantial farming business at Swainby, which is today owned and operated by his eldest grandson, Steven Dawson. Eleanor soon handed over her business activities and Maurice became the Managing Director.

By 1980, now with an 11 acre site, the haulage fleet was increased by the acquisition of another Teesside haulage business, WG Thomas Ltd, which raised the number of vehicles to 60.

A Heavy Haulage division had been part of the fleet since 1972, now in 1980 Dawsons introduced its biggest tractor unit yet, a Scania capable of pulling 150 tonnes. To complement the tractor a

Top left: A Volvo heavy haulage tractor with a King rear steer low-loader, transporting storage tank sections through Ripon in the late 1960s.
Above left: A Dodge 7.5 tonne lorry with swap body furniture van. Right: Heavy haulage vehicle 145 Scania with Nichola 6 axle hydraulic trailer carrying 100 tonnes of teset weight blocks, 1980.

the first of three which would be run on the site. To commemorate the occasion Vernie was presented with a model 0800 locomotive by the Managing Director of British Rail.

The following year Margaret Thatcher's government abolished the National dock Labour Scheme; with that gone Dawsons was able to extend its stevedoring activities to cover all aspects of shipping other than wet bulk cargoes.

Vernie Dawson, the company founder, sadly died in 1990 shortly after his 70th birthday.

Following Vernie's death the company embarked upon building its first concrete quay which was completed in 1991. Over the next seven years the wharf saw substantial growth handling import and exports on behalf of many customers with tonnage rising to over 400,000 tonnes a year.

Since that time the company has had its share of ups and downs: in 1998 British Steel moved its exports to Teesport resulting in a massive fall in business for Dawsons with just 12 weeks notice. Amazingly as a result of winning other business only two redundancies were required and later that year an £800,000 extension to the Ayrton Railhead would be opened by the junior minister for transport Michael Strang.

Also in 1998 the Company took the huge step in purchasing the adjacent offshore fabrication yard known locally as Linthorpe Dinsdale, now renamed North Sea Supply Base. This has enabled Dawsons to discharge larger ships of up to 7000 tonnes and has extended the quay frontage to 900 metres. The huge white fabrication halls on this site are visible throughout Teesside.

New people were brought in to the firm to carry on the drive for success which had so characterised

Vernie's attitude over the years. Now Gary Dawson, grandson of Vernie and Eleanor was promoted to Managing Director whilst Maurice Dawson took over the position of Chairman having been Managing Director since Vernie's 'retirement' 25 years earlier.

Early in 2000 the company bought new tractor units and a number of new trailers and the firm's transport fleet was back in business proudly displaying the company emblem that Vernie had developed 50 years previously - the Dawson Shield.

Sadly Eleanor was not to see the new fleet having died in February 1999 shortly after her 80th birthday.

At the beginning of the new millennium the future looked bright for AV Dawson with Corus requiring a railhead in the north east to receive and deliver its South Wales tonnage whilst at the same time Terra, formerly ICI, required help to rail transport its products to its Avonmouth factory.

Now with 55 acres of property, over 300,000 sq ft of warehousing, lorry fleet, railhead, wharfage, cranage up to 600 tonnes capacity and numerous items of mechanical handling plant and equipment in support, and a staff of 60 people AV Dawson have come an awful long way since that day in 1938 when Vernie Dawson spent his hard earned £50 to buy Dina and her cart.

Above left: *A Guy tractor unit with 180hp Cummins engine delivering grouser sections on behalf of BS Skinningrove in 1966, Dawsons still work for the same mill today, now owned by Corus.* ***Below:*** *Chairman, Maurice Dawson and Managing Director, Gary Dawson pictured in the conference room of the new administration building at the Ayrton Railhead.*

A century on the tiles

Where would we be without a roof over our heads? Pretty wet and miserable that's where. For thousands of years people have tried to make their homes watertight using whatever materials came to hand. The poor would use thatch, the better off baked tiles or slates made from local stone whilst our cathedrals and great houses were roofed in lead sheeting.

The locally available materials used by the vast majority of people gave each area of the country a distinctive look. In the 19th century with the spread of the railways that situation began to change. Slate quarries in north Wales found they had a market for their products which was no longer restricted to the Welsh mountains but now encompassed the whole of Britain. Nor were the Welsh the only ones to benefit, Westmoreland, Cumberland and Lancashire grey slating also became a familiar sight in roofs from Lands End to John O'Groats. And of course in Middlesbrough.

WB Robinson is an old family established business founded in 1898 by the unusually named William Brass Robinson. The company was initially founded to carry out repairs of roofs coupled with the distribution of New Welsh Slates from premises which were located directly opposite the old goods yard. The full business name in those days was WB Robinson, The North Eastern Slate Works, North Road, Middlesbrough; WB Robinson advertised himself as 'slate merchant, slater and tiling contractor'. Limited company status and the sons would

Above left: *WB Robinson.*
Below: *A Robinson family photograph.*

come much later. Slates were brought in by train from Wales and were then re-distributed by WB Robinson originally using a horse and cart. The company still owns the premises of the old stabling where the horses were kept. The natural progression from mainly slate distribution was into the fixing of slates and the supply of other roofing material such as damp proofing materials and slate 'undercloaks' and the small firm soon branched out.

The majority of staff lived locally; they usually started in the firm from school and were put through an apprenticeship of five years before becoming a slater. In those far off days staff were still called 'men' whilst owners were still known as 'master' a distinction later replaced by the more democratic sounding 'employers' and 'operatives'.

Working hours in those early days which saw the death of the Queen Empress Victoria were 6.30 am to 5pm from February through to November and from 8 am until 4,30 in the darkest months - all for just tenpence per hour, old money or four pence in today's decimal equivalent.

Slates were not the only type of roof the firm became involved in. When the built-up felt roofing system was developed WB Robinson was the first local company to train its staff to lay felt in hot bitumen using coal fired boilers. The skill was not only in laying the roof but also in lighting the boiler and keeping it at the correct temperature to heat the bitumen. The tradesmen selected to be trained in that

side of the roofing business were originally good labourers who were struggling with age to meet the physical demands of carrying heavy roofing materials. Happily for them these men were trained in felt roofing and in due course this eventually became a major part of WB Robinson's roofing business.

William Brass Robinson passed the family business down to his three sons, two of whom Harry and Herbert Hyde Robinson worked in the business. George, the third son, went by himself but retained shares in the company.

The company continued in operation throughout the course of the first world war, the short-lived boom which followed it and the great economic depression of the 1930s. Life was never easy and one of the worst periods came during the second world war when the firm lost a lot of men who either joined the armed forces or left to work in other aspects of the war effort.

During those years the firm was under severe pressure to make roof repairs after bomb damage but with many slaters away fighting, meeting demand was not easy. Shortage of all materials and with new replacement products causing problems after fixing merely compounded the frustration.

Top: A WB Robinson memo dated 1919.
Above: A quote from WB Robinson to a Messrs WA King & Sons Ltd, 1918.

Fortunately most men returned after the war to carry on as slaters, and some had been highly decorated because of their bravery in battle; conquering a fear of heights whilst working on roofs had perhaps contributed to their brave conduct during those terrible times.

After the war years had settled the business was passed to George William Robinson, Herbert Robinson's son who had come out of the RAF and proceeded to carry on his training as a slater working out on the roofs alongside the men. Eventually George William, known throughout the building industry as Bill Robinson, took over the business and became Managing Director overseeing the practical side of the roofing work. When Bill's own two sons James and Herbert left school they followed him into the family company, and like their father before them both training out on the roofs on all aspects of roofing. Both brothers would admit that this period was one of the most enjoyable time of their training, especially as they were working with and under some of the old slaters who were always willing to offer their experience - and in some cases a heavy hand when the need arose.

On the death of Bill Robinson his two sons James and Herbert took over the running of the company. In the early days of that period a new road system was put in which for the first time allowed all sizes of vehicle to the yard entrance whereas before the only way past the railway lines, locally known as 'The Border', was under low level bridges or over a single level crossing which had made road access fairly difficult. The new road system gave good access for both supplies and sales and following the purchase of surrounding properties in the early 1980s a sales side of the firm, the Cleveland Roofing Centre, was opened with Mike Read in charge.

This was a time when many builders were beginning to carry out their own roofing work rather than sub contract to specialist slaters.

The work had been made much easier with the introduction of modern materials. The sales side grew very quickly and a further depot was opened in Newcastle, though run directly from Teesside. The two sides of the company grew hand in hand, but the sales side was always Mike Read's section of the business with Jim and Bert Robinson specialising in the traditional side of roofing. During this period the company was working throughout Britain roofing as far away as Scotland and London; the company's reputation for fine work was such that when in 1990 Eton College needed a roof overhaul Robinson's was selected for the job. The long term contract meant completing a section of the College roof each year, a project which was still ongoing more than ten years later.

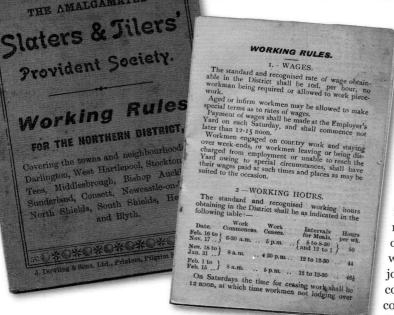

Top: A Labour Price List of 1902.
Above: The cover and first page of the Slaters & Tilers Working Rules circa 1900.

have contributed to the success of the firm; David and his brother Richard, David's wife Alison, David's father-in-law Ted Veal and David's two sons, David (Jnr) and James.

been based at its present location, Bolckow Road, Grangetown. A satellite office was opened at Immingham on South Humberside in 1991, run by Don Rooney who had been with the firm since 1972.

In the early days, however David worked alone, operating a van hire business and undertaking emergency express deliveries up to 1 tonne working for Smiths Docks Co. Ltd at South Bank and Shell Oil at Teesport Refinery. At that time the business was based at the premises of R & I Raby on Snowdon Road, Middlesbrough, referred to by locals as Over the Border until more suitable premises could be found. These were days involving long hours. David had to keep appointments and also try and increase the range of clients. But growth came very quickly.

In 1970 the company had taken over the Acklam Road Service Station next to the Coronation Hotel. Here there was ample parking space as well as fuelling and servicing facilities for the light vans and commercial vehicles he was operating at the time. A year later there was another move - to larger premises in Stonehouse Street, Linthorpe village. This was the year that he was able to purchase five articulated vehicles and trailers - these were kept and maintained at the old Andersons Foundry at Port Clarence. Since 1976 the company has

A significant development occurred in 1979 when the Executive Coach business was launched. This brought David's sister, Alison into the business. Following the success of this new line of business David's brother, Richard joined the company in 1983. Richard, who was 19 at the time, had been an apprentice footballer with Middlesbrough during the reigns of Jack Charlton, John Neil and Bobby Murdoch.

Top left: A David Fox van from the 1970s.
*Top right: David's sister Alison after learning to drive their 'Old Dolly' 1934 Baby Austin 7. **Above:** Enjoying a glass of bubbly, David Fox (left), Nigel Shaw, David's wife Alison and David's sister Alison (far right).*
***Below:** A David Fox award winning coach of 1979.*

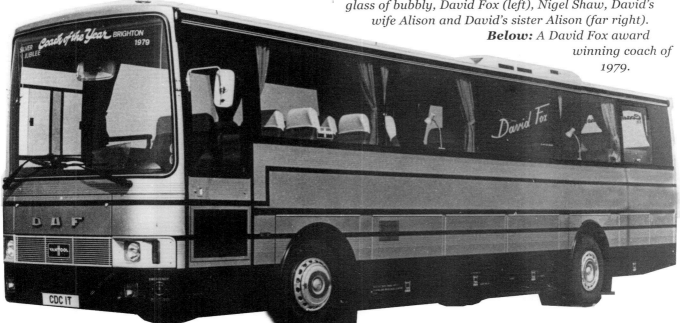

Annual Coach of the Year Show at Brighton and won the 'Coach of the Year Award' along with several other silver jubilee trophies. The coach was the first of a new breed in coach travel and made the realisation of an entirely new experience for coach passengers possible. Only those who have travelled long distances on uncomfortable, cramped coaches with nothing better to do than try and read magazines until the next coffee stop, could appreciate the revolutionary nature of this first class coach.

Having acquired this vehicle at great cost, the firm was able to offer a first class service for travelling celebrities and that is how Neil Armstrong and Genesis came to be transported on David Fox coaches. This led to another exciting development when the firm secured contracts to be involved in the movement of staging and scaffolding equipment for European tours of music groups such as the Rolling Stones, Genesis, Bruce Springsteen, Queen and Michael Jackson. One such contract was with a group called John Watts and Para Music - a happy coincidence as John Watts was the name of the man who drove their coaches for many years, and who has played his own special part in the success of the company.

Throughout its history David Fox Transport has always made a priority of being equipped with an up-to-date and well

It was under Jack Charlton that Middlesbrough Football Club became Second Division Champions. To celebrate the occasion David Fox Transport provided a tractor unit and 40ft trailer made up to look like a football pitch. Unfortunately the level of excitement in the local population increased to such an extent that the trailer had to be taken away when boys started climbing on it as it was parked outside the Evening Gazette offices.

The company acquired a chassis cab through Bill Beadnell of Brian Sharp DAF Trucks Ltd, Billingham and arranged for the manufacture of a special body and interior for it by Van Hool Ltd, Europe's principal coach builders. On completion in 1979, the coach was presented at the 25th

Top left: Richard Kirby, Accountant (left) and Alex Fox Managing Director and Chairman of Cleveland Tankers Ltd. Top right: The crew of the 'Rolling Stones' tour.
Above left: David Fox Transport advertised at a 1980s match between Middlesbrough and Ipswich Town. Left: A David Fox Trailer unit. made up as a football pitch to celebrate Middlesbrough's Second Division Championship.

maintained fleet. New vehicles are regularly purchased to replace older ones.

Today David Fox Transport is a family run, medium sized road haulage business specialising in the transport of steel, newsprint and chemicals throughout the UK.

Throughout its history, commitment, service, quality and training have been the core values behind the company's success. They will also form the bedrock of future developments. They have been awarded the prestigious BS EN ISO 9002:1994 accreditation. All their vehicles are serviced regularly in-house by their skilled fitting staff who man the Grangetown depot 24 hours a day, Monday to Saturday. All long distance vehicles are equipped with 'In-Cab' telephones and some drivers are trained in Hazpack regulations. Transport managers, operators and office staff all have a comprehensive, long-standing knowledge of the industry and can instantly help with any distribution problems. Alongside those previously mentioned are other long-serving staff members such as Nancy Truran, Company Secretary, who joined the firm in 1972, around the same time as Don Rooney. Both Nancy and Don are good friends of the Fox Family. Barry Mitchell, who served his apprenticeship with David Fox Transport, Charles Dryden, Bill Filer, Linda Stockell, Pauline Taggart and Dawn Hoggarth, and some long-serving drivers such as John Cubbin, Brian Thompson, Ged Stebulitis, Terry Barker and Reg Gant to name but a few.

There is an ongoing need for training and David Fox Transport has its own facilities offering individual training courses for forklift trucks, gantry cranes and other relevant topics. These courses are open to the general public and other businesses. They have been used by hauliers, crane and engineering companies and local councils. The company's philosophy is to grow steadily and maintain a good customer base built on reliability of service without resorting to cut price tactics in a shrinking marketplace.

This philosophy has stood the firm in good stead over the years and has led to the success which it enjoys today. It has helped the company weather some major storms

over the years, in particular the closure of two of its main customers in the Middlesbrough area, namely Shell UK at the Teesport Refinery and Smith Docks Ltd at South Bank and Haverton Hill. Since these closures there has also been the virtual end of ICI Billingham and the closure of several steel plants as well the changes at ICI Wilton. But enjoying a wide customer base the firm looks set for continuing success in the future.

*Above left: A Fox heavy goods vehicle. **Above right:** David Fox being presented with the keys to the first four Iveco Ford Tractor Units to enter the David Fox Transport Fleet. The presentation was made by Bill Beadnell, Chairman of North East Truck and Van Ltd. **Below:** David Fox with wife Alison and Sons David Jnr (left) and James.*

Stepping out in style

Middlesbrough residents were the first people to benefit from the footwear offered by the Clinkard Group which now has branches all over the country. The company's success has been based on offering the customer what he likes to wear. This has proved to be a potent recipe for success.

It all began in 1924 when Charles Clinkard decided to utilise the experience and expertise he had gain by managing a branch of Stead and Simpson and Robinson's Footwear in the town by going into the footwear trade on his own. So with the assistance and support of his wife, Eveline, he put his best foot forward, as it were, and started the business.

Premises were rented at 19 Corporation Road, Middlesbrough and Charles and Eveline began to offer a valuable service, stocking good quality shoes at a good price, and paying particular attention to the fit of shoes, especially in the case of children. This philosophy proved to be very successful.

There was a great deal of optimism in the early 1920s. Many were seeking to put behind them the horrors of the 'war to end all wars' and felt that better times were ahead. It was a time also when wealth was beginning to be more evenly distributed and 'ordinary people' had higher aspirations. It seemed an auspicious time to be in business but the buoyant mood did not last

Top left: *Founder, Charles Clinkard.*
Left: *Charles Clinkard's first advert which appeared in the North-Eastern Daily Gazette on Thursday April 24th 1921, the day before he opened his first shop.*
Below: *The original shop, 19 Corporation Road.*

rationing during and following the second world war. Footwear was at a premium and they were able to sell any stock they could acquire, such was the shortage at this time.

They aimed to supply Middlesbrough families with medium to high grade footwear. They prided themselves on their extensive product knowledge which enabled them to offer a valuable service to their customers.

The period after the second world war, especially after the use of clothing coupons had come to an end, had seen the company expand steadily, both in terms of the number of shops it has and the kind of trade it pursued.

long. The General Strike of 1926 had a devastating effect on businesses and long weeks without wages meant that hundreds of local families had nothing to spare for anything but the most essential items of clothing. Many businesses went bankrupt and the Clinkard's were in only their third year of trading.

Somehow they weathered the very difficult era of the 1930s and better times were to come, 1938 found the business in good shape. Charles was able to secure the purchase of the property next door but one, 16 Corporation Road, and was set to benefit from the demand for affordable, quality footwear during the years of deprivation and

By this time, Charles and Eveline's sons Colin, Jon and Roger, were involved in the family firm and brought their own contributions to the business.

The second branch of Clinkard's was opened in the High Street in Stockton-on-Tees and this was the start of an expansion which has seen the Clinkard name in town centres throughout the north-east and far beyond. Nowadays there are branches as far afield as Sheffield, York, Leeds, Bristol, Milton Keynes and Guildford.

Top: *The interior of 19 Corporation Road.*
Above left: *Charles Clinkard and his wife Eveline.*

Charles Clinkard lived to see the start of this expansion programme before he died in 1964 and had the satisfaction of seeing the company placed on a secure footing. The firm had become a limited company in 1953, his sons had been able to benefit from learning from him many fundamental lessons about how to run a successful business, which were to stand them in good stead in the years to come.

It was in the mid-1960s that a major re-fit of the Middlesbrough store took place, many readers will probably remember this. Something that is less generally known is that a new line of business commenced for the Clinkard family when Intershoe Ltd was set up, originally to bring seal-skin boots from Norway into the UK.

was opened in Leeds. The following year the company opened their flagship retail outlet at Eldon Square, Newcastle upon Tyne and Clinkard's became a well recognised and respected regional name, selling not only shoes but also accessories under the Elizabeth Anne name.

The firm has had a continued commitment to offering the right product at the right price at the right time - a philosophy which required an impressive administrative back-up to achieve. In addition staff training has always been a feature of the Clinkard way of doing things and the tradition of offering personal service has continued throughout the firm's history, remaining as important now as it was back in the 1920s.

During this time the expansion programme was also going ahead with new shops at Northallerton and a move from Station Road to High Street, Redcar. In 1975 the first branch outside Teesside

The 1980s and 1990s were a time of great change and development for the firm with branches opening in prestigious malls in nationally renowned shopping centres such as Coppergate, York, Meadowhall, Sheffield, Cribbs Causeway, Bristol, and Trafford Park, Manchester. This reflects company policy of opening shops in all key retail locations in the UK.

Above: *The shop front decorated to mark the occasion of the Jubilee of King Edward.* ***Left:*** *Eveline Clinkard and son Roger meet England's 1966 World Cup winning captain, Bobby Moore (centre).* ***Bottom left:*** *A fashion show on the 50th Anniversary of Charles Clinkards.* ***Below:*** *A family photograph on Eveline Clinkard's retirement after 52 years in the shoe retail trade.*

In a highly competitive market, Clinkard's have found their niche and are offering the public shoes which they want to buy. Though Charles Clinkard senior would possibly find it hard to comprehend the extent of his family's business, he would be gratified to know that the family and their dedicated staff have achieved their success by following the very principles which he started out with; affordable quality and personal service.

Clinkard's also have a wholesale operation which supplies well-known departmental store names such as Selfridges, the John Lewis Partnership among others, as well as supplying stores run by Clarks and Start-rite.

Clinkards has also opened a number of factory outlets. The first one was in Hartlepool, which opened to the public in 1994. Since that time further factory shops have been developed in Hatfield, Stoke and Clacton as well as two further outlets in Scotland. They also have a specialist branch in Guildford.

Over the years the company has benefited from securing the services of gifted people who have been able to contribute in various ways to the firm's success at all levels. Customers are invariably more familiar with the sales staff and they represent the 'front-line' operation, as it were. However there have been numerous people over the years who have provided marketing and administrative support without whom the Clinkard success would not be what it is today.

This is certainly an impressive record of achievement and has been gained by following a customer-oriented policy. Clinkards believe that the customer is always right - well, most of the time anyway. Their buyers are instructed to meet public demand and not necessarily buy what they personally like.

The business is continuing the family tradition to the third generation with grandson Charles, now in the position of Group Managing Director.

So what of the future? Though details may be unknown at present, it is certain that Clinkards will continue to look ahead and seize opportunities to expand to other areas and provide a truly nation-wide service. They have certainly proved beyond reasonable doubt that they are providing a valued service to the public by offering a good product at a reasonable price. This has served them well in the past and will doubtless continue to do so in the years ahead.

Top: *Charles Clinkard's Middlesbrough shop in 1971.*
Above left and below: *Two of Charles Clinkard's shops in Meadowhall, Sheffield.*

A sporting life

When Middlesbrough lad Paul Barry became the new owner of the renowned Jack Hatfield Sports shop back in 1999 he knew he was taking on not simply a shop but part of the town's heritage.

The business was founded before the Great War of 1914-18 by Tom Hatfield, the father of Jack G Hatfield, one of Teesside's greatest sporting heroes.

It was in 1912 that Tom Hatfield opened his sports shop in 6 Newton Street. That year his son Jack won two silver and one bronze medal at the Stockholm Olympics for his freestyle swimming. The following season Jack would break three English swimming records and four world records and would astonishingly go on to compete in both the 1920, 1924 and 1928 Olympics.

Before his death in 1965 Jack Hatfield had been a director of Middlesbrough FC for thirteen years, an association which would continue for two more decades with his firm continuing to supply the football club with all its equipment and clothing. After Jack's death he was honoured by having a town square near Fry Street named in his honour.

But meanwhile what of the business? The shop had moved to 39-41 Borough Road only in 1970 having remained in Newton Street since its opening in 1912. Following his father's retirement from the business Jack Hatfield had run the shop; during the first world war however Jack was in the Army in France and his sister Bertha joined the business - and stayed until 1933! Later Jack's sons Jack junior, Peter and Tommy would join the firm, with the younger Jack eventually becoming general manager, Peter running sales and purchasing and Tommy taking charge of sales and deliveries.

All kinds of sporting goods were and continue to be supplied: tennis, soccer, rugby, cricket, squash, badminton, swimwear, snooker, billiards, darts, indoor games, table tennis, judo, fencing, archery and riding wear. Not even the interruption of the second world war could slow trade due to the large stocks held at the war's outset and the necessary ability to repair goods as well as sell them.

One service which used to be offered until the mid 1970s was inflating leather footballs. Up to a hundred balls a week were inflated for customers, although the service was not offered on a Saturday when handling the old-fashioned muddy dubbin-coated footballs would have made it difficult for staff to deal with customers wanting crisp white sports clothes.

Both pictures: *Teesside and England sporting hero, Jack Hatfield.*

The latest owner of the sports shop, Paul Barry, is no newcomer having previously had a 30 year link with the business and having been its manager for 15 of those years. Paul first worked for the Hatfield enterprise in 1969 and except for a two year break would remain with the business from then on.

Today the shop stocks 50 different styles of snooker cues and dozens of different style of darts. The shop also stocks the unusual - anything from a croquet set to a lacrosse stick.

From behind what is the longest traditional counter of any shop in Middlesbrough, staff are proud of their reputation for being able to provide almost everything which can be thought of in the sporting arena - though not everything bought is used for sport: British Steel has bought referees' whistles for use in the shunting yards, whilst bladders, once used in footballs have been used by ICI and the gas industry for gas testing.

Perhaps the greatest testimony to the legacy of Jack Hatfield is the loyalty of customers, some famous, others humble amateurs who simply want the best. Most come to the shop in person, others who are now ex-patriots regularly send in orders by post and over the telephone. Today grandparents bring in their grandchildren to buy from a firm where their own grandparents brought them when they were children.

And there are the famous clients, especially well known soccer players. They call in for a natter, and invariably leave with some item of equipment; and they leave behind their names in Paul Barry's bulging autograph book. But however well known they may be though it is doubtful their names will ever be as celebrated as the one above the door.

Above: Jack Hatfield pictured with a selection of his trophies. Left: Jack Hatfield with sons Jack jnr (back right), Tommy (front left) and Richard, 1965. Below: Jack Hatfield jnr, 2001.

From handcart to hi-tech shopfitting

A Middlesbrough company which aims to provide unequalled service, competitive pricing and quality craftsmanship has found this to be an enduring secret of success. Hills' Interiors and Construction Ltd of Stonehouse Street, Linthorpe has been serving the local community and beyond for well over a hundred years and is set to succeed in the future.

In 1887 Joseph Henry Hill established a family business decorating the grand houses of Victorian Middlesbrough. The firm's reputation for quality work and high standard of craftsmanship started to grow form the beginning.

Though the business today is very different from what it was in 1887 there is still some continuity with the past. Nowadays many of the specialist techniques such as graining, ragging and sponging which were in vogue during the Victorian era are today in demand by hotels and pubs in achieving an authentic traditional look. Hills' craftsmen are still able to provide this valued service.

Joseph Henry's expertise was nurtured through the middle part of the 20th century by the second generation of the Hill family, Tom Hill, who guided the business to its early industrial contracts for firms which were developing in the area, such as ICI British Steel and Boots chemists, the licensed trade and a local supermarket chain.

Today Hills' Interiors and Construction Limited is run by Roland Hill, the grandson of the founder.

Much has changed since Roland used to help out in the family's wallpaper shop as a Saturday boy and drive the company's van

Above: Founder, Joseph Henry Hill (left) and son Tom.
Below: JH Hills' original shop in Newport Road.

keep up with this give them a cutting edge compared with much of the competition.

A proactive and receptive management team recognises the need for prompt and efficient design solutions and the value of a partnership approach with clients and consultants to achieve budget targets and product quality.

The firm has a well-equipped in-house joinery workshop which can offer tailor-made solutions to clients' requirements. The company's concern to keep at the forefront of the field is demonstrated by its commitment to using renewable timber wherever possible. Their clients include such big household names as Asda, Safeway and K.F.C-Kentucky fried chicken. At the turn of the century it was successful in winning a contract worth over £1m to restore the Arndale shopping centre in Manchester, which bore the brunt of the IRA bombing several years ago. They were also pleased to win the contract to refurbish the public rooms of Middlesbrough's Thistle Hotel.

delivering decorating materials to each contract. He can remember when starting work in 1960, it was common to see the company's craftsmen pushing handcarts around the town.

The company now has experience in the fitting out of major construction projects including Shopping Centres, Hotels, licensed premises, supermarkets, and offices and the manufacture of architectural joinery. Hills are now capable of handling contracts measured in many millions of pounds.

Spearheading its way in the modern competitive environment with Roland Hill are Wayne Holmes, the senior estimator and David Thompson, contracts manager. Other personalities include Christina Cordell, the finance manager and Clare McMahon administration manager, who both have been with the company many years.The core site and workshop number is around 40 but this can increase dramatically during certain big contracts. As the company expands new managers and permanent staff will be employed

Hills' tradesmen are fully trained to comply with all Health & Safety regulations. There is a constant need for updating on techniques and training, and Hills' ability to

Though many things have changed over the years, Joseph Henry would still give his nod of approval to the standards Hills' still continue to maintain.

Top left: *Roland Hill pictured with the van he drove when joining the family business at the age of seventeen.*
Right: *Third generation and Managing Director Roland Hill, 2001.* **Left and below:** *Interiors fitted out by Hills. Below is the bar area of Middlesbrough's Thistle Hotel.*

A *steely eyed business*

A Middlesbrough company which has extended the scope of its expertise from the immediate locality as far as South America was started in 1926 by Hugh Crosland and the twin Parson brothers. Claude and Clyde.

They went into business to sell iron and steel materials and they soon had offices, in London, Birmingham, Manchester, Glasgow, Swansea, Brussels and Middlesbrough. They also diversified their activities, buying out companies and offering management consultancy and long term loans to finance business.

During the world wide slump in the early 1930s offices had to close, directors' fees were cut and the two Parson brothers resigned, leaving Hugh Crosland as sole Managing Director. At this time, the Head Office was in River Plate House in the City of London and H Henderson was the Chairman.

The group's first dealings in South America were through Kenneth Henderson who opened the first office in Buenos Aires in 1926. This foothold in a foreign market proved an advantageous move as in those days it was difficult for foreign companies to get credit from European suppliers and Parson & Crosland acted as a confirming house.

In 1935 Evans Thornton became a limited company and Parson & Crosland took 40 percent of the shares in return for their existing Argentina businesses, namely Philco and Lindley engineering. Philco Argentina is now one of the largest manufacturers of televisions and video recorders in the country.

After the end of the second world war there was a shortage of steel. In 1948 the company moved out of River Plate House. Things were difficult on the home market but Evans Thornton had a bumper year in 1947 due to the sale of 100 Gloster Meteor Jet Fighter aircraft for the sum of £4 million, the first aircraft of the Argentine airforce.

Top left: Hugh Crosland. Left: Lionel Butler Henderson and colleagues at work in South America. Below: A Parson & Crosland custom built vehicle for travel to remote locations by railway track.

In 1966 the company bought the Newport Works (its present site) from Richard Hill and sold its lifting gear business. The following year Sir Charles Fitton died. In 1968 Ian Crane was made General Manager, becoming a director in 1977. At this time the non-ferrous foundry of William Lane was bought, having been established by the Lane family in 1863.

By 1974, the year the office moved to Kingsway, London. Portman Hill moved to Middlesbrough and Parson & Crosland (Middlesbrough) Limited was formed.

Evans Thornton was wound up as a holding company in 1978 after a break-up of the directors. The firm now owned a non-ferrous foundry Sacima (sold in 1996), the aircraft sales company Aviesta as well as some agencies which ceased trading after the Falklands Conflict of 1982. Aviesta is now involved in the automation business and sells robots and quick release couplings.

In 1995 Charles Crosland was killed in a riding accident and Ian Crane became Chairman and Managing Director of the group. One year later an offer was received from the firms partners in Peru and Parson & Crosland's shares in Crosland Tecnica were disposed of.

Back in the UK, the Middlesbrough office was run by Charles (later Sir Charles) Fitton, who was made a director of the company in 1933. Almost the whole of the business was involved in the stocking of steel and iron. In those days this was not very sophisticated - in many cases a stockist had steel leaning against the walls of his warehouse the ends of bars sunk into a channel in the ground. Bars were simply pulled away when required. Today stocks stand at around 6,000 tonnes, most of which are heavy structural steels.

Although the Group has changed its shape over the years, the main core business, of steel stock-holding and processing, continues to grow and develop through investment in added value and the development of new markets.

In 1948, Hugh's son, Charles Crosland joined the company and was almost immediately sent to work in Argentina.

Top left: A Parson & Crosland exhibition in 1968.
Top right: Parson & Crosland's transport fleet, 1966.
Below: Parson & Crosland's premises, Forty Foot Road.

The 1950s was a time of expansion due to acquisitions. In 1951 Teesbank Ltd was bought in Middlesbrough, specialists in the testing and repairing of wrought iron, steel chains, wire rope slings and general lifting gear. This year also marked the 25th anniversary of the founding of the company and one week's pay was awarded to the whole company.

Towards the end of the 1950s Charles Crosland and some Peruvian contacts formed Peru Mercantil, a trading company which started selling Rolls Royce Diesel engines. Later this company was to become Crosland Tecnica.

Caring for your car

Park Lane Garage is a familiar sight to the people of Middlesbrough, many will have stopped to fill up with Esso petrol on its forecourt and many will also have benefited from the expertise of the Millers who own it and who have been responsible for the many repairs and MOT tests throughout its history. The garage has been at these premises since George Miller, father of the present owner, founded the business in 1947. George had served in the Royal Air Force - he was stationed at Thornaby during the Second World War and decided to invest his time and efforts in the garage venture once peace was established.

It was an inspired move as the motor car was about to come into its own. A car still a real luxury in 1947, was to become the realisable goal for what are often called 'ordinary' people to purchase. And perhaps no-one at that time could have foreseen the enormous volume of traffic which is our daily experience on the roads of all our towns and cities. It is certain at least for the foreseeable future that car maintenance will be an extremely valuable means of making a living.

And who can imagine that selling petrol will become obsolete? George Miller entered into an agreement with the Esso company and Park Lane Garage has been selling this brand of petroleum products throughout the existence of the garage, it is now the only Esso garage in Middlesbrough and the only local one with attended service, the Millers are very proud of this long-standing tradition.

At the beginning George offered the usual range of garage services, mechanical repairs, body repairs, but he was also a skilled coach builder and was the

Above: Where it all began, a view of Park Lane in the 1940s. *Below left:* Crashed and damaged vehicles used for parts and body repairs. *Below:* Park Lane Garage 1947.

they are no different from anyone setting up and running their own business, but whatever financial headaches there have been the business has steadily prospered and grown.

Though the garage has never moved from its original site, the Millers' share of it has not always been so great. They were able to extend by purchasing adjacent land which allowed them to build a showroom and petrol forecourt. Subsequently they were able to acquire two other local parts outlets and now are the largest independent parts supplier in the area.

They seek to offer their customers a personal and quality service at competitive prices and over the years have built up good relations with many customers who have confidence in their expertise and return time and time again for petrol and repair services provided at the garage.

As ever looking to the future there are plans to give a corporate identity to all three parts outlets and to develop a company website. These initiatives will serve to build on the solid business foundations built up over the years by the Miller family.

first on the Middlesbrough scene to offer a recovery service for crashed vehicles. Repairing crashed cars he needed a stock of spare parts which he also offered direct to the public.

Top left: The garage forecourt in 1952.
Above left: Dennis Miller clearing up debris after vandalism to the garage. *Below:* Park Lane Garage, 2001.

It has always been very much a family affair, initially George did the garage repair work and his wife, Ann, saw to all the administrative tasks. Nowadays the repair side of things is the responsibility of their son, Dennis who is pleased to be able to carry on the good work started by his father. They have always kept up-to-date with the latest equipment to carry out their work as efficiently and well as possible.

It has not all been plain sailing though, there have been a number of times in the last sixty years when cash flow has been a problem - in this

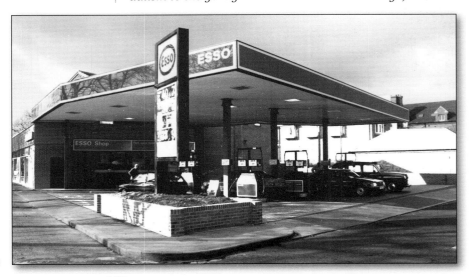

The sweet taste of success

Liberato Greco was born in Arpino, just south of Rome. This little town was the birthplace of Cicero but Liberato decided that the ice cream industry, not the oratory, would be where he would devote his energies. Maybe he had too many rivals in Italy, but for whatever reason, in 1907 he and his brothers, Antonio and Tullio came to the UK. Here he began to sell ices, first from a hand barrow. Soon he graduated to a horse and cart and later still to a motor bicycle and sidecar.

In the early 1920s, having learned his trade from a Middlesbrough employer, Liberato decided to set up in business on his own in Suffield Street. After a year or two a change was made from making ice cream to manufac-

turing wafers and cornets. In all these enterprises, Liberato was helped by Antonio and Tullio. The work was hard, involving as it did, the use of manual

methods of manufacture and the hours were long. But their hard work paid off and provided a living for themselves and succeeding generations of the family. Liberato's daughter, Hilda, learned her father's trade and demonstrated the same attitude of commitment as Liberato and his brothers had done.

War-time is invariably an occasion for families to suffer loss of loved ones and the Greco family are no exception and the family has had its share of sadness and heart-ache. During the Second World War the male members of the Greco family were interned. The three brothers were travelling aboard the Andorra Star as internees, bound for Canada, when the ship was torpedoed by a German U-boat and sank in mid-Atlantic. Five hundred miles out from Ireland, a destroyer, the St Lawrence, picked up survivors who had been adrift in the sea for over six hours. Sadly one of the brothers, Tullio, was lost in the cold waters. The St Lawrence returned all survivors, including Liberato and Antonio, from the Andorra Star back to Britain.

Here Liberato's daughter, Hilda, had been capably running the business for him in his absence, and Liberato was able to take over the reins of the business once more. A few years later Hilda married a fellow Italian, Laurence

Above left: *Founder, Liberato Greco, 1926.*
Left: *Liberato in his Model T Ford, Albert Park.* ***Below left:*** *Batter mixing, 1952.* ***Below:*** *Tony Rovardi pictured in the early 1950s.*

Antonio Rovardi, who has made his own valuable contribution to the firm. The couple's sons, Peter and Lawrence, continued the family tradition of running the business to the third generation. Lawrence, incidentally, was so named after the ship which picked up his grandfather and great uncle during the war. Now Peter's son, Tony is currently learning the role filled by Lawrence up to his recent retirement, making the business a four generation concern.

To survive, companies have always to keep up with new technology and other developments in their field. In 1980 the company was looking towards modernisation and expansion, so a move was made from its original premises in Suffield Street to the company's present modern factory location in Greta Street. Nowadays, using state of the art cone and wafer ovens, the firm manufactures products to sell to many wholesale ice cream manufacturers and retail outlets throughout the UK.

The product range these days is far more extensive than in the past. The customer is almost spoilt for choice confronted with the delights of thick and crispy chocolate wafers, nougat wafers, oyster shells, sugar cones, twin cones and single cones in a variety of sizes as well as many other products used by the ice cream trade.

Due to increased demand the factory premises have been extended to include the land previously occupied by Middlesbrough School. Part of the Old School Complex, as it is known, is rented out to other local businesses as well as incorporating the enlarged cone production area and storage facility.

Perhaps many of us have enjoyed Greco Brothers' products without being aware of it. That the company with humble beginnings has survived and grown so much over the years is a fitting testimony to the commitment and dedication of the Greco brothers and the succeeding generations of the family.

Top: A selection of Greco Brothers cornets, wafers and biscuits. *Above left:* Liberato with his grandson Lawrence. *Below left:* A view inside the Greco Brothers warehouse. *Below:* Peter and Lawrence exhibiting at an ice cream convention.

Steely ambition

These days it is somewhat unusual to find a thriving modern company still firmly in the hands of the family which founded it. But that is the way things are at steel stockholders SM Thompson Ltd. The present Managing Director Howard Thompson is the son of Stanley Moorhouse Thompson who began Steel Stockholding at Port Clarence in 1950.

There have been many changes since then - an early move to the present more accessible site at the Marathon Works near Newport Bridge and the continuing updating of plant and equipment such as the 'Profiler' and its magic eye that can cut any shape, any size in lengths of steel plates up to 10 metres - and cut up to six profiles simultaneously. Despite massive changes in technology however the family tradition remains and is reflected in the way the firm approaches customers. As for the future the firm is looking forward to an ambitious expansion drive increasing the stock and machinery.

Stanley Moorhouse Thompson set out in business for himself after flying with RAF bomber Command during the second world war following which, for three years, he worked in the offices of a local steel stockist. Like many young men Stanley had long been nursing an ambition to be his own boss. For most the dream would remain a pipe dream, but for those few with the drive to succeed that ambition would become reality.

Having gained experience Stanley took office space in Lloyds Bank Chambers. He began buying and selling steel on his own account from works at the old railway station Port Clarence on the other side of the Tees and using the Transporter Bridge to get there from his office.

Stanley's wife Lilian helped him in those early days acting as company secretary; Howard Thompson, Stanley and Lilian's eldest son joined them in 1963. The firm moved to its present location, then surrounded by terraced houses, in 1966. The surrounding streets have long since disappeared but in those days the area was densely populated.

Stanley had a strong feeling for people around him whether they were his employees or not, knowing that it was difficult for local people to get into town at Christmas to see the lights Stanley even provided a Christmas tree each year for the local children to see.

At the new site Stanley built an office block and works warehouse, installing guillotines for cutting mild steel plates and sections, overhead cranes and named the whole the Marathon Works, a reflection of Stanley's long-standing interest in athletics.

Above: Founder Stanley Moorhouse Thompson and wife Lilian, 1949. Below left: The company's first lorry outside their 1950s works at the Old Port Clarence Railway Station. Below: Stanley Moorhouse Thompson meeting HRH Prince Charles in 1977.

Howard Thompson became managing director of SM Thompson Ltd in 1982. He is an accomplished horseman and over the years has competed in show jumping, team eventing, national hunt and point to point racing. The firm's other director is Derek Thompson, Howard's younger brother a presenter and commentator for Channel 4 Racing.

Today the firm sells to structural engineers and manufacturing industry across the United Kingdom as well as exporting to the Netherlands, Hong Kong and Sweden.

Top left: *The Thompson family and members of staff, Cannon Street, Christmas 1956.* ***Top right, both pictures:*** *Director Derek Thompson (left picture on the right) and brother Howard Managing Director (right picture), presenting to winners at a Channel 4 race meeting.* ***Above left:*** *A staff picture from the 1950s.* ***Below:*** *A view inside Marathon Works.*

Amongst his many interests Stanley Thompson was well known as an athletics official with Middlesbrough and Cleveland Harriers and was often seen, microphone in hand, giving quite literally 'running commentaries' on local and national athletics events and agricultural shows.

Stanley was to become President of the Northern Counties Cross Country Association in 1963/64 and in 1978 became vice-chairman of the Captain Cook Appeal Trust raising funds locally and overseas for the building of the Captain Cook Birthplace Museum in Stewarts park Middlesbrough. Stanley was also Secretary of the Cleveland Point to Point for many years.

Nor were sports Stanley Thompson's only interests outside the world of steel. Singing was a part of his life too. Stanley was also Chairman of the Apollo Male Voice Choir organising their visits overseas and Chairman of the Middlesbrough Amateur Operatic Society as well as being an enthusiastic member of the Middlesbrough Rotary Club.

Stanley Moorhouse Thompson died in 1983. His wife Lilian was still company secretary in 2001; until 1986 she been involved in local government for more than 25 years having been an Alderman and Deputy Mayor and she is still a governor of two local schools and a trustee of the Captain Cook Museum.

A growing business

Are green fingers passed down the generations through the genes? Judging by the experience of Norman Wall, founding proprietor of Cherry Hill Nurseries in Stokesley Road, Hemlington the answer must be, 'Yes'. He left his job as a metallurgic chemist in the early 1950s to concentrate on being a landscape gardener and ran the business from an allotment also used by his parents who ran a floristry business and grew dahlia and chrysanthemums there.

In 1964 Norman moved to the present site when the allotments were sold for building. The new location was a two acre site which, when the Walls first saw it was extensively under water. There were a couple of sheds and a house on it. The name of Cherry Hill Nurseries was decided upon and three pink flowering cherry trees were planted on the roadside. However on one occasion only a couple of years after the nursery was opened an overzealous member of staff pruned them so hard that the trees failed to recover. They died and somehow no one ever got around to planting replacements.

Norman used the sheds for storing his landscaping equipment and set about the difficult task of reclaiming the land. He initially grew plants he needed for his landscaping contracts but as new houses were built nearby there opened up an opportunity to sell them direct to the public. Both plants and the business started to grow from then on.

Over the years additional land was purchased to accommodate the development of the business and now the nursery extends across a five acre site. As in interior design and clothing, so in gardening, fashions come and go. Roses were all the rage in the 1960s and 1970s and Cherry Hill Nurseries would take orders for thousands of rose trees ready for autumn planting. Nowadays the emphasis is on low-maintenance gardening and shrubs and heathers are popular. Dramatic architectural plants such as palms, bamboos and grasses are in vogue among the gardening public, often planted among coloured gravel.

There is an increasing demand for plants suitable for the patio; decking and water features are also very well liked.

Above: *Norman Wall, founder of Cherry Hill Nurseries.*
Below: *Cherry Hill as purchased by Norman Wall.*

provide all the accounting and administrative support.

They feel that their main strength is that they offer a personal service to their customers, putting all the knowledge of plants which they have acquired over the years at their customers' disposal. They are always seeking to satisfy clients' demands and plan in the future to extend their second greenhouse, increase their range of patio pots and open a coffee shop.

Cherry Hill is now called a Garden Centre which marks the availability of so many non-plant items on sale but still retains the designation 'nursery' to emphasise the fact that the foundation of their expertise is with things that grow. Their business proves this to be the case.

Norman saw his business put on the way to real success before he died in 1992 and his family are still very much involved with consolidating its past and promoting its future success. The Garden Centre is run by his two daughters, Janet Summers and Judie Livingstone and Norman's son-in-law, Paul Stamp, runs the landscape gardening side of things. They have recently been joined by a member of the third generation connected with the business when grand-daughter, Claire Summers came to work in the shop which has been recently opened to sell gardening sundries and furniture. Norman's wife Edie continues to

Above: An Aerial view of Cherry Hill in the 1970s.
Below left: Norman Wall pictured in 1989.
Below: From left to right, Claire Summers, Paul Stamp, Janet Summers and Judie Livingstone in the entrance to Cherry Hill Nurseries Ltd Garden Centre, 2001.

In the 1960s both government and the general public were anxious about the threat of nuclear war. Major powers had arsenals of nuclear warheads aimed at each other, capable of delivering a payload that was sufficient to destroy cities or nations in one strike. Both the communist states and the 'anti-red' factions feared each other's strength, leading to a stand off known as the cold war. There had been some nervous moments, especially when America and the Soviet Union pushed each other to the brink in the 1962 Cuban missile crisis, and when President Johnson sent GIs into war in Vietnam. At home the talk was of four minute warnings, the Campaign for Nuclear Disarmament marches and atomic rain. Civil defence exercises, just as meaningful as those of 30 years earlier, were undertaken, just in case of nuclear attack. Firemen at Acklam Lower Wharf took part in a drill on 30 September 1966, imagining that an atom bomb had been dropped on Middlesbrough. It was a water borne exercise inter brigade initiative, in which the only place to escape the holocaust and devastation was a small region in the ironmaster's coop, to which there was no access by road.

Going to law

The long-established local firm of solicitors Atha and Co was founded by Tony Atha who, in 1958, had qualified as a solicitor after having served five years as an articled pupil with Messrs. Sykes, Johnston and Lee solicitors of York.

After serving a two year stint of national service, as an officer in the Army, Tony Atha was admitted as a solicitor of the Supreme Court of Judicature in 1960. He was fortunate to be then almost immediately offered the opportunity by his old firm to set up a new office in Redcar as a partner with his former principals. In Redcar the practice of Sykes, Lee and Atha had the main responsibility of servicing the conveyancing requirements of a large building firm called Bradley Builders (York) Ltd.

Over a period of three years in a small first floor office suite in Redcar, and with the assistance of one secretary, Tony Atha conveyed over 300 properties on the Ings Farm Estate; and during that period he also acquired a good number of private clients. When the

Above left: *Company founder, Tony Atha.*
Below: *Atha & Co's premises in Middlesbrough.*

estate was completed, as per a previous arrangement with Tony's partners, they vacated the partnership and left him as sole principal in the practice, which was now renamed Atha and Co.

Tony Atha's first builder client, Bradley Builders, had been delighted with the work carried out on its behalf. When the building firm moved onto open sites in Scarborough, York, Marske-by-the-Sea and Stockton-on-Tees it invited Tony Atha to carry out the legal work in the development of these estates on the basis that he would open a local office to deal with each estate.

> *The Middlesbrough office would eventually employ five qualified solicitors, four experienced fee earners and a support staff of 30*

Assistant solicitors were recruited and soon Tony Atha became the common partner in a number of individual partnerships established in Redcar, Marske-by-the-Sea, Skelton in Cleveland, Middlesbrough, Scarborough, Guisborough and York. The already established practices of Cress Tarn Stockton, Eagle Clark and Co. Filey and Clifford Smith in Burnley, Lancashire were

Above: *Atha & Co's Middlesbrough office seen from another aspect.*

subsequently acquired to complete a network of 12 offices all serving local building sites developed by Bradley and Co.

Regrettably the building firm got into financial difficulties in the late 1970s and was no longer a source of business; fortunately however the individual practices and their local partners had by then become sufficiently well established to survive without their main source of business.

In the early 1980s Tony Atha's son Charles took his degree in law and decided to serve his articles with the Newcastle firm of Ward Hadway. Whilst at that time Tony Atha was disappointed that his son chose to serve his articles with another firm it proved to be the right decision since it gave Charles an insight into fields of legal work not practised by his father's firm.

On qualifying and being admitted as a solicitor Charles Atha decided to come back and join his father who gave him charge of the Middlesbrough office which was then staffed by an Assistant Solicitor, two fee earners, three secretaries, a receptionist and a book keeper. In the mid 1980s Tony Atha decided to retire from his individual partnerships and sold out his interest to his then partners. Some of those now ex-partners proudly retained the Atha name in their firm's titles such as Atha, Strong & Co at Marsk, Atha Summers and Co at Scarborough, Atha Barton and Co at Guisborough and Evans, Atha and Co at York.

Tony Atha continued to look after clients, who were personal friends, from his office adjoining his home in Saltburn whilst also assisting his son in the conveyancing side of the business at Middlesbrough.

Atha & Co became one of the first firms of solicitors in England to become a corporate body recognised by the Law Society

Charles, meantime, developed an interest in personal injury work and industrial disease claims and the Middlesbrough practice expanded rapidly to service that work. The growing Middlesbrough office would eventually employ five qualified solicitors, four experienced fee earners and a supporting staff of 30 and enjoy an annual turnover of more than a million pounds.

Moving ever forward Atha & Co became one of the first firms of solicitors in England to become a corporate body recognised by the Law Society.

The industrial disease and personal injury side of the practice built up steadily. Over a period of ten years or so the firm settled in excess of 15,000 industrial deafness and other related injuries for the people of Teesside recovering some £30 million in compensation. Eventually however the industrial disease work began to decline and the firm began to concentrate solely on personal injury claims. The firm successfully marketed a 'no win no fee' scheme and was years ahead of local competition in Middlesbrough. The firm likes to think that it constantly keeps at least two steps ahead of competitors whilst offering clients the best possible funding arrangements.

Atha and Co became the first firm of solicitors on Teesside to market itself on radio, and it would later move into television advertising, competing head to head with the various claims management or 'claims farming' companies which were springing up and attracting so much bad publicity when some deducted huge amounts from clients' compensation.

By contrast Atha and Co's aim has always been to provide the client with a first rate service and to secure the maximum possible compensation.

By far the greater majority of new business comes via recommendations from satisfied clients, something which the firm believes is the best form of advertising.

The rules of the Court concerning personal injury claims changed significantly in the closing years of the 20th century and it became essential to specialise exclusively in that field, failing which practitioners would simply be unable to keep up.

Meanwhile the effect of increasing competition from non-qualified claims management companies which advertised widely would be to significantly expand the market for personal injury claims by alerting potential clients to make a claim when they previously would not have bothered; but such firms also challenged the traditional solicitor by competing ferociously for clients.

It remains to be seen whether claims management companies will continue to be a threat or whether they will melt away as quickly as they arrived.

To maintain its position however Atha and Co recognises that it is essential for it to focus on client care, ensuring that it provides a sound financial deal within a fair and flexible 'no win no fee' agreement. They just get on with the job.

Right: *Tony Atha's son, Charles now taking the firm forward into the 21st century.*

Youngsters making good use of the Children's Library in July 1949.

Acknowledgments

The publishers would like to thank
Larry Bruce, Senior Librarian (Special Projects) at Middlesbrough Central Library

Thanks are also due to
Andrew Mitchell who penned the editorial text
and Judith Dennis and Steve Ainsworth for their copywriting skills

A major problem for the company would be a shortage of skilled labour to maintain its high standard of workmanship, a problem made far worse when the apprenticeship system came to an end.

The company's current staff have all been trained within the company, many of the trainees having learned alongside Jim and Bert. The sales side would eventually be sold to allow the original company to specialise in what it does best, the fixing of roofing materials. This has meant that the company's offices have moved from its original premises, which are still owned by WB Robinson & Sons, to a small industrial unit in Edith Street on the Letitia Industrial Estate, approximately one mile up river. Robinson's however remains in close contact with the Roofing Centre for the majority of its material.

Today Robinson's mainly concentrates on specialised roofing on all types of buildings but particularly listed buildings roofed in original and traditional materials.

In the firm's early days it used the advertising slogan 'Above all a good roof'. Roofs are a vital element of any type of construction and should only be fixed or repaired by skilled tradesmen. Robinson's tradesmen are second to none and are backed by a company with more than a century of experience in the business. 'Above all a good roof' maybe, but behind that good roof you'll find WB Robinson & Sons Ltd.

Above: *The National Association of Slate Merchants and Slaters handbooks from 1899 and 1903.*
Below: *Current owners Bert and Jim Robinson, both represented Middlesbrough and their County as Rugby players.*

Delivering the goods

Anyone keen on puzzles may like to ponder the following; what have Neil Armstrong (the first man on the moon), the pop band Genesis, and a model of a football stadium in common? Answer: they have all been taken to their destinations by David Fox Transport.

The company which owns and operates a mixed fleet of high quality vehicles was founded by David William Fox in 1969. He was fortunate to be able to call on the advice and guidance of his father, Alexander Ballantyne Fox who had his own personal experience of the haulage industry, having worked for R Rankin & Son. It was Alex who negotiated with T D G plc, who owned R Rankin, permission for David to enter the transport arena on the condition that he did not go into direct competition with the Rankin business. Alex made another vital contribution to his son's fledgling business in the form of a £750 loan. This money enabled David to purchase second hand vans and mini buses to lease. It was given as a loan but Alex never asked for it back - though it must also be said that David never actually offered to repay it either!

Close family involvement has been a feature of the company. In addition to Alex's initial input a further three generations

Top left: *Founder David Fox.* **Above:** *David Fox pictured in front of one of his first vans, 1970.* **Below:** *David Fox outside his first garage, 1970.*